MODERN WORLD CULTURES

Africa South of the Sahara

Australia and the Pacific

East Asia

Europe

Latin America

North Africa and the Middle East

Northern America

Russia and
the Former Soviet Republics

South Asia

Southeast Asia

This is what the Earth looks like at night. This image is actually a composite of hundreds of pictures made by orbiting satellites. Man-made lights highlight the developed or populated areas of the Earth's surface. The dark areas include the central part of South America, Africa, Asia, and Australia.

(Credit: C. Mayhew and R. Simmon; NASA/GSFC, NOAA/NGDC, DMSP Digital Archive.)

MODERN WORLD CULTURES

Australia And The Pacific

Elizabeth J. Leppman

Series Consulting Editor
Charles F. Gritzner
South Dakota State University

CHELSEA HOUSE
PUBLISHERS
An imprint of Infobase Publishing

Cover: Crowds take in the sun and surf at New South Wales, Australia

Australia and the Pacific

Chelsea House
An imprint of Infobase Publishing
132 West 31st Street
New York NY 10001

ISBN-13: 978-0-7910-8150-1

Library of Congress Cataloging-in-Publication Data
Leppman, Elizabeth J.
Australia and the Pacific / Elizabeth J. Leppman.
p. cm. — (Modern world cultures)
Includes bibliographical references and index.
ISBN 0-7910-8150-8 (hard cover)
1. Australia—Juvenile literature. 2. Oceania—Juvenile literature. I. Title. II. Series.
DU96.L46 2005
994—dc22

2005010040

Series and cover design by Takeshi Takahashi
Composition by MCC
Cover printed by Yurchak Printing, Landisville, Pa.
Book printed and bound by Yurchak Printing, Landisville, Pa.

Printed in the United States of America

This book is printed on acid-free paper.

TABLE OF CONTENTS

INTRODUCTION

Charles F. Gritzner

Geography is the key that unlocks the door to the world's wonders. There are, of course, many ways of viewing the world and its diverse physical and human features. In this series—MODERN WORLD CULTURES—the emphasis is on people and their cultures. As you step through the geographic door into the ten world cultures covered in this series, you will come to better know, understand, and appreciate the world's mosaic of peoples and how they live. You will see how different peoples adapt to, use, and change their natural environments. And you will be amazed at the vast differences in thinking, doing, and living practiced around the world. The MODERN WORLD CULTURES series was developed in response to many requests from librarians and teachers throughout the United States and Canada.

As you begin your reading tour of the world's major cultures, it is important that you understand three terms that are used throughout the series: geography, culture, and region. These words and their meanings are often misunderstood. **Geography** is an age-old way of viewing the varied features of Earth's surface. In fact, it is the oldest of the existing sciences! People have *always* had a need to know about and understand their surroundings. In times past, a people's world was their immediate surroundings; today, our world is global in scope. Events occuring half a world away can and often do have an immediate impact on our lives. If we, either individually or as a nation of peoples, are to be successful in the global community, it is essential that we know and understand our neighbors, regardless of who they are or where they may live.

Geography and history are similar in many ways; both are methodologies—distinct ways of viewing things and events. Historians are concerned with time, or when events happened. Geographers, on the other hand, are concerned with space, or where things are located. In essence, geographers ask: "What is where, why there, and why care?" in regard to various physical and human features of Earth's surface.

Culture has many definitions. For this series and for most geographers and anthropologists, it refers to a people's *way of life*. This means the totality of everything we possess because we are human, such as our ideas, beliefs, and customs, including language, religious beliefs, and all knowledge. Tools and skills also are an important aspect of culture. Different cultures, after all, have different types of technology and levels of technological attainment that they can use in performing various tasks. Finally, culture includes social interactions—the ways different people interact with one another individually and as groups.

Finally, the idea of **region** is one geographers use to organize and analyze geographic information spatially. A region is an area that is set apart from others on the basis of one or more unifying elements. Language, religion, and major types of economic activity are traits that often are used by geographers to separate one region from another. Most geographers, for example, see a cultural division between Northern, or Anglo, America and Latin America. That "line" is usually drawn at the U.S.-Mexico boundary, although there is a broad area of transition and no actual cultural line exists.

The ten culture regions presented in this series have been selected on the basis of their individuality, or uniqueness. As you tour the world's culture realms, you will learn something of their natural environment, history, and way of living. You will also learn about their population and settlement, how they govern themselves, and how they make their living. Finally, you will take a peek into the future in the hope of identifying each region's challenges and prospects. Enjoy your trip!

Charles F. ("Fritz") Gritzner
Department of Geography
South Dakota State University
May 2005

CHAPTER 1

Introducing Australia and the Pacific

Australia, New Zealand, and the many island groups in the southern Pacific Ocean all feel the effects, in one way or another, of the world's largest ocean, the Pacific. To reach these places, various groups of settlers had to cross that ocean in whole or in part. Its currents affect the climate, and vacationers swim in its waters. We often refer to this region as "Oceania," and in this book we refer to it as Australia and the Pacific. Nevertheless, this region is very diverse; the ocean affects the lands in different ways.

The cultural region formed by Australia and the Pacific involves a huge swath of the Earth's surface. Australia is about as big as the United States, without Alaska and Hawaii, and it is a continent in its own right. About 1,300 miles (2,100 kilometers) to the southeast lies

This is a view of the outback at Kata Tjuta, Northern Territory, Australia. Australia and the islands of the Pacific have a wide variety of geographic environments, including the deserts of Australia and the tropical rain forests of New Guinea.

New Zealand, an island country about the size of Colorado. The eastern half of the island of New Guinea, making up the country of Papua New Guinea, lies north of Australia and is a little larger than California. (The rest of the island of New Guinea is part of the Southeast Asian country of Indonesia.) The smaller islands in the Pacific Ocean are often divided into three groups, based on cultural differences recognized by early European voyagers to the region. Nearest to Asia are the largest islands, forming Melanesia, from the Greek words for "black" (melanos) and "islands" (nesos) because the people there have dark skin coloring. Micronesia, from "small" (micros) and "islands" (nesos) is to the north of Melanesia and includes the Marianas, the Marshall Islands, and the Federated States of Micronesia. Polynesia ("many islands") stretches to the east as far as Easter Island.

Islands have been grouped together for purposes of governing, in some cases rather arbitrarily for the convenience of former colonial rulers. Palau, Federated States of Micronesia, Marshall Islands, Nauru, Kiribati, Solomon Islands, Tuvalu,

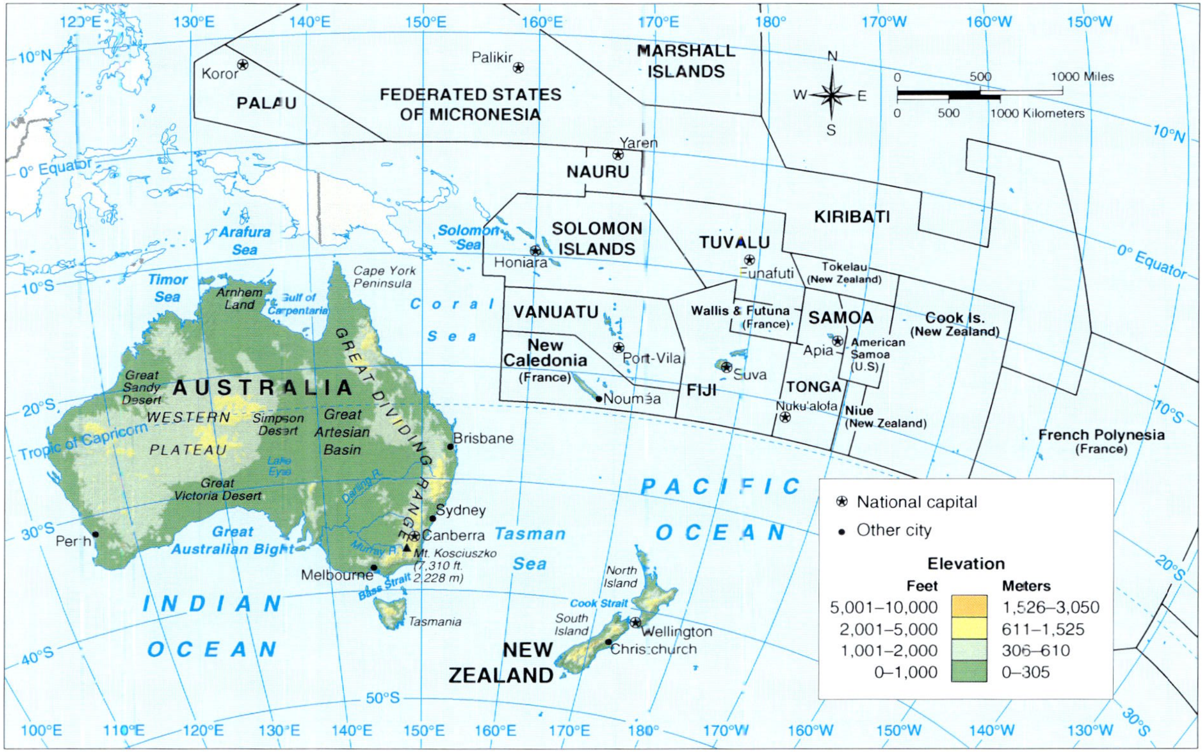

This reference map of Australia and the Pacific islands shows the countries, cities, and major landforms of the region. Australia is about the same size as the continental United States.

Samoa, Tonga, Fiji, Solomon Islands, and Vanuatu are independent countries. The United States controls Wake, Northern Marianas, Howland, Baker, and Palmyra islands. French Polynesia is still French, as are New Caledonia, Wallis, and Futuna. New Zealand rules the Cook Islands, Tokelau, and Niu. Pitcairn is British, and Easter Island belongs to Chile. Australia and New Zealand were once British colonies, then became dominions (internally self-governing), and today are independent countries that maintain ties to the British monarch and the Commonwealth. Papua New Guinea was governed by Australia on behalf of the United Nations after World War II and then became independent in 1975.

All these countries and islands, large and small, together stretch from 110° west longitude (Easter Island) to about 110° east longitude (western Australia), and from about 21° north latitude (Northern Marianas) to about 47° south latitude (Southwest Cape, New Zealand). To put it another way, when it is noon on Easter Island, it is 3:00 A.M. the next day across the international date line in Perth, Australia. On the same day, weather may range from tropical warmth on Baker Island almost on the equator to a snowstorm on South Island in New Zealand. Papua New Guinea receives rain all year and has tropical rain forests, whereas central Australia is a desert.

Location also helps create the region's distinctiveness. It is about as far away from Europe and North America as you can get on Earth. Yet, many of its people maintain ancestral, cultural, social, and business ties to those regions. People in the Northern Hemisphere often call Australia and New Zealand "Down Under," because they are so used to seeing maps and globes with north at the top. Looking at a globe this way almost gives the impression that people in those countries are standing on their heads! Of course, that's a false idea because "up" and "down" refer to "away from" and "toward" the center of the Earth, and Australians and New Zealanders are standing on the Earth just like people anywhere. Before World War II,

Europeans and North Americans referred to East Asia as the "Far East," and Australians and New Zealanders adopted that point of view. However, World War II in the Pacific Ocean quickly demonstrated that the East Asian "Far East" was really the "Near North." Today these countries are part of the Pacific Rim, building trade and other connections with their Asian neighbors to the north. They have also received many immigrants from Asia since the 1970s.

Like the Americas and Africa south of the Sahara, Australia and the Pacific were unknown to Europeans before the Age of Exploration. Europeans had an idea that there must be land in the Southern Hemisphere to "balance" the continents they knew, but that was just a theory. Australia and New Zealand were among the last parts of the world to be explored and settled by Europeans because the distances—and the dangers—to reach them were so great. Even though Europeans had done a lot of exploring before they explored the southern Pacific Ocean in detail, there were many dangers, high adventures, and heroes involved in learning about this part of the world. The crew of the *Bounty* mutinied because they felt so abused; the mutineers settled on Pitcairn Island. The officers that they overthrew made their way back to England after facing dangerous waters and starvation. Explorers died in the deserts of interior Australia. Crossing the huge ocean without places to obtain fresh food caused sailors to develop a disease called scurvy, until doctors found that lemon or lime juice (which is rich in Vitamin C) would prevent it.

Before Europeans began to settle Australia, New Zealand, and the Pacific islands in the late 1700s, all these places had native populations who had lived there for hundreds, even thousands of years. As they did in the Americas, Europeans took land from the indigenous (original) peoples and drove them to less desirable parts of the countries, as the newcomers developed agriculture, mining, and other enterprises. In the Pacific islands especially, they brought other people to work in these enterprises, and their descendents remain. Europeans and Americans also sent missionaries to convert the native peoples to Christianity. Today, the countries differ in their relationships between the descendents of the indigenous peoples and the settlers, and these relationships remain important issues for the peoples of these countries.

Australia was first settled by prisoners from England. The government sent them there because the land was so far away. This view that dangerous people could be sent to Australia and be too far away to cause any trouble continued well into the twentieth century. Today, with modern jet aircraft, this region is not quite so isolated (and Australia is no longer a nation of convicts). Because it is still quite a distance, even when one is flying, however, Americans still think of going there as a once-in-a-lifetime venture.

European settlers in the Pacific islands needed to find a way to support themselves and develop a lifestyle that they remembered from their homeland. This was their definition of success. They might find mineral wealth, or they could develop farming and ship those products back to Europe in return for the manufactured goods they wanted. Early settlers generally became farmers; only later was the great mineral wealth of Australia discovered. Some Pacific islands also had minerals that could be exported; others produced farm crops like sugar and coconuts. In any case, this region has always had a global outlook, as it has always relied on trade to make a living.

Australia and New Zealand's European residents achieved independence from Britain in the early twentieth century without fighting a war. In Australia, the different colonies united in a federation, and the British Parliament declared the country a dominion. A dominion handles its own internal affairs, but Britain continued to be responsible for relations with other countries. Australians and New Zealanders fought in World War I and World War II alongside British forces. Now the countries are fully independent, and each makes its own decisions. Australia joined the United States in the war in Vietnam and in the invasion of Iraq, whereas New Zealand did not. The smaller Pacific islands became independent after World War II, and some are still tied to colonial rulers. Many are dependencies of Australia and New Zealand through the Pacific Forum. With small land areas and small populations, their role in world trade and politics remains small.

In general, Australia and the Pacific is a peaceful region, generating few world crises. Consequently, we hear very little about the region in the media. Nevertheless, these countries have fascinating histories and cultures. They face some of the same challenges that the United States does, and their approaches to meeting these challenges may offer suggestions to Americans about how to meet some of their own problems.

CHAPTER 2

Natural Landscapes of Australia and the Pacific

Think big! Both the landforms and the climate of Australia and the Pacific relate to gigantic forces that affect the entire Earth. Different locales support very different kinds of plant and animal life. Long periods of evolutionary isolation have also produced some unique life forms.

FORMATION OF THE LAND

The region of Australia and the Pacific includes huge contrasts in landforms—from an entire continent to tiny oceanic islands. Australia and the continental islands owe their existence to movements of huge tectonic plates, whereas the oceanic islands arose from the floor of the Pacific Ocean.

Shape of the Land

On the time scale of a human lifespan, the location and outlines of the continents seem stable. If we expand our vision to a geological time scale, encompassing millions of years, however, we find that they are constantly shifting.

Until about 200 million years ago, Australia (including New Guinea) and New Zealand formed the southeastern-most part of a huge supercontinent that geologists call Gondwanaland. To its northwest was the southern part of Africa, and to its west was Antarctica. The mountains of eastern Australia match those in Antarctica, and the curved coast of Wilkes Land in eastern Antarctica fits into the southern coast of Australia.

About 200 million years ago, the supercontinent began to break up, and the various pieces, called tectonic plates, began to move slowly over Earth's surface. The centers of these huge plates are quite stable. It is at the edges of the plates that things get interesting. The tectonic plates collide with other plates, and something has to give, because there is only so much room on the planet. Some of the rock on that edge of the plate gets pushed down into the crust and mantle, and is heated to become molten again and so recycled.

Under such enormous pressure, the edges of the plates also buckle and crumple, like a small rug pushed against a wall, but with much more violence. The plates colliding and slipping past each other, horizontally or vertically, causes earthquakes. Lava may be forced to the surface, and volcanoes erupt. Thus, the world's major mountain ranges and deepest ocean trenches are found along the edges of the tectonic plates, where this crumpling and subduction (pulling of the crust downward) have taken place. All around the Pacific Ocean, plates being pushed by sea-floor spreading in other parts of the world collide with the Pacific Plate, causing earthquakes and volcanic eruptions—the famous Pacific "Ring of Fire."

Australia, including the island of New Guinea, remained attached to Antarctica until about 55 million years ago. The collision of the Indo-Australian Plate (which also carries India) with the Pacific Plate produced the mountains of Papua New Guinea and nearby islands. These areas experience earthquakes and volcanic eruptions to this day, and New Zealand's Auckland boasts beautiful scenery that is based on remains of volcanoes.

The continent of Australia, however, is the lowest and flattest of continents. The mountains that formed at the edge that collided with the Pacific Plate are in New Guinea and nearby islands, and New Guinea became separate from Australia when the sea level rose after the last Ice Age (about 10,000 years ago). Australia's highest point is Mt. Kosciusko at 7,313 feet (2,229 meters), which is the lowest of the highest peaks of the world's continents (about half the height of higher peaks in the Rocky Mountains, Sierra Nevada, and Cascade ranges of North America). Almost all of Australia is the center of a plate composed of ancient hard rock and not subject to the forces of plate collision. The Kimberly Plateau in the northwest is the remains of an ancient mountain range that has crumbled, revealing rich minerals. In the center of the country are the MacDonnell Ranges, and south of them, the world's largest monolith, Uluṟu, or Ayers Rock. Its origin is uncertain, but it may be the hard sandstone that remained when surrounding rocks eroded away.

These ancient, hard rocks are rich in minerals, and, in Australia, these minerals were exposed by erosion. There are deposits of gold in the Kimberly Plateau in northwestern Australia as well as around the Gulf of Carpentaria, in the southeastern state of Victoria, and on the island of Tasmania. Less exciting, but more useful to industry, are the rich iron mines of the state of Western Australia, and copper, lead, zinc, bauxite (the ore for making aluminum), nickel, and manganese. There are also deposits of precious and semiprecious stones like opals, for which Australia is famous.

Fuel resources in Australia are the remains of ancient plant and animal life. Therefore, they are found in rocks that were formed in later periods in geological history than the ancient

The origin of the world's largest monolith, Ayers Rock (also called Uluru), is uncertain. It may be the hard sandstone that remained when the softer surrounding rocks eroded away.

cores of plates, after life had appeared on Earth. Most often, these rocks were originally formed from layers of mud or remains of sea life that, over time, were compressed into rock. Some of these layers were later uplifted by tectonic activity, often where tectonic plates collided. Consequently, it is not surprising to find that most of Australia's coal deposits are in the Great Dividing Range along the country's east coast. Newcastle is a big coal-exporting port, named for a city in England that is also famous for its coal. Australia's few petroleum deposits are in a basin filled with these sedimentary rocks west of the Great Dividing Range. Deposits off the northwest coast are related to the petroleum deposits of Indonesia. The fuel resource found in the ancient rocks of interior Australia is uranium, the fuel for nuclear energy.

New Zealand has very little of these types of resources. For many millions of years, it was probably part of the seafloor east of Australia, at the edge of the Indo-Australian plate. Scientists think it separated from Australia about 60 to 80 million years

Steam rises from Geyser Flat at Rotorua's geyser field in Rotorua, New Zealand. The tectonic plates located below New Zealand are spreading apart. Geysers and hot springs form when lava issues out of these cracks in the Earth's crust. Heat from the lava causes water to boil and steam to rise to the surface.

ago, when the Tasman Sea formed, but for many long eons, it was at best a series of small islands. The country's present form is the result of geologic processes that took place over only the last 100,000 years or so, most of them related to volcanic and earthquake activity. South Island represents the upwelling of lava where the Indo-Australian and Antarctic plates are moving apart and enough lava has accumulated to form dry land. Mineral wealth is limited to minor coal, oil, and gas deposits. New Zealand does, however, have hot springs and geysers, or geothermal (earth-heat) energy, when water comes in contact with hot lava and rises to the Earth's surface. Whole towns can be heated and supplied with hot water from these springs, and New Zealand has been in the forefront of developing this type of energy. Most activity is found in the north-central part of North Island, with Rotorua the most famous site. With abundant precipitation and mountainous terrain, New Zealand also has great potential for hydroelectric power.

The southern, flatter region of Papua New Guinea harbors the same kind of rocks as Australia, and there are copper deposits in the central part of the island. Similarly, petroleum has been found in the sedimentary rocks that have been laid down on the older foundation. Papua New Guinea probably hides additional minerals, but much of the island has not been explored in detail by geologists. New Britain (which is part of Papua New Guinea), the Solomon Islands, Vanuatu, and New Caledonia are the tops of mountains of the same range as the mountains of northern Papua New Guinea; of these, only New Caledonia has mineral wealth, in the form of nickel.

The movement of tectonic plates continues, and the collisions cause earthquakes and volcanic eruptions. In 1995–1996 and again in 1999, for example, Mt. Ruapehu on New Zealand's North Island erupted, spreading ash and dust for miles and interfering with air travel. New Zealand suffers frequent earthquakes. The Indo-Australian Plate is moving north at the rate of about 3 inches (8 centimeters) per year. Geologists believe that in another 50 million years, at the end of the Psychozoic ("knowing life") era, it will have shifted north so that New Guinea will be off the east coast of China, and Australia will lie astride the equator.

The Pacific Islands

The large continental islands—New Guinea and the islands of New Zealand—as well as Samoa, Tonga, and Fiji, lie on the junction between the Indo-Australian and Pacific plates, but the smaller oceanic islands are all on the Pacific Plate. They come in two varieties: high volcanic islands that are really the tops of volcanoes that sit on the ocean floor, and low coral atolls. Both begin as volcanic eruptions deep under the ocean.

Scattered across the Pacific Ocean are "hot spots" where lava reaches the seafloor, the surface of Earth's crust. If enough lava accumulates over the hot spot, it appears above the surface of the ocean as an island. (An undersea volcano called Lo'ihi located off the southern coast of the island of Hawaii will probably become a new island some day.) These volcanic islands provide beautiful scenery and fertile soil as well as beaches of fine sand—sometimes black in color.

Various kinds of coral live in the warm waters around the island. Over time, these coral build huge structures from their bony spines. Coral is rock-hard and comes in many beautiful colors, the most famous being pink and white. It can also be black; black coral is the state rock of Hawaii. As coral accumulates in the warm, calm waters off the shores of landmasses or on undersea mounts (submerged mountain tops), it forms barriers to boats trying to reach the islands. The most famous example is the Great Barrier Reef off the northeastern coast of Australia, the largest coral formation in the world and one of Australia's major tourist attractions. Smaller islands have also found that coral reefs attract visitors, but Pitcairn Island, settled by mutineers from the ship the HMS *Bounty*, is still hard to reach because of coral reefs offshore.

Even as the coral reefs are growing, the volcanoes that form the cores of small islands may erode. As the Pacific Plate shifts location and the hot spots stay put, the islands are carried away from the source of lava that builds them. Rain and wave action erode the islands, and eventually they may disappear under the surface of the ocean. The coral rings that have formed around them remain and may grow, however, even though they may never get very high above sea level. Coral can also grow on volcanoes that remain slightly below the level of the sea. Inside the ring- or horseshoe-shaped atoll is a lagoon. The largest atoll in the world, Kwajelein Atoll in the Marshall Islands, is 80 miles (130 kilometers) long and 19 miles (30 kilometers) wide; its lagoon covers 612 square miles (1,600 square kilometers). In the

1950s, the United States and other Western governments used some of these atolls to test nuclear weapons because they were too small to be populated but were large enough on which to set up the apparatus for the testing.

WEATHER AND CLIMATE

With such a range in latitude, we expect the climate in various parts of Australia and the Pacific islands to be very different. This is, in fact, the case: The Pacific islands and Papua New Guinea are warm all year, whereas South Island of New Zealand has real winter, with enough snow for skiing.

Global Climate Patterns

The variation in climate patterns depends, first, on latitude. The sun's rays are most directly overhead and thus bring the most energy within a band 23 ½° north and south of the equator. The place where the sun's rays are directly overhead moves north and south through these low latitudes with the changing seasons.

Where the sun's energy is most concentrated, the heated air rises and cools, and the atmosphere is cooler the higher you go. Eventually, the air gets cold enough that it cannot hold its moisture, and it rains. Thus, places near the equator, including Papua New Guinea and the nearby Pacific islands, have warm, rainy weather all year.

In December and in June, the sun's greatest energy falls at the Tropic of Capricorn (23 ½° south latitude) and the Tropic of Cancer (23 ½° north), respectively. Those locations then receive heavy tropical rains. Rain follows the sun. Places that will get this rainy season at the opposite time of year are dry when the sun is lower in the sky during its daily passage. This tropical wet-and-dry climate is typical of northern Australia.

To the north and south of the tropical lands are places where it rains very little; some years may receive no moisture at all. Around 30° north and south latitude are the world's great deserts, including those that cover most of Australia.

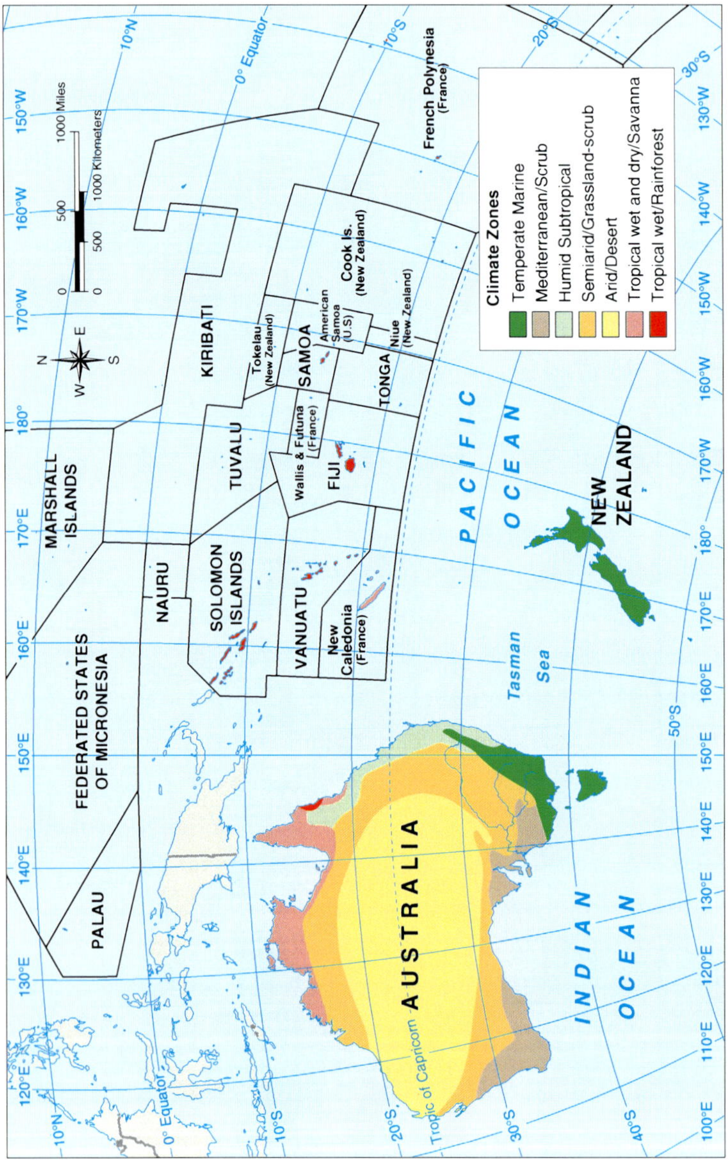

The majority of the small islands in this region lie in a tropical zone, between the equator and either the Tropic of Cancer or the Tropic of Capricorn. New Zealand is farther south and has a temperate marine climate. Because of its size, Australia has various extremes in climate including the tropical northern coast, the temperate marine climate of the southeastern coast, and the vast desert interior.

As we move farther from the equator, the next rainy area is the belt of the westerlies, so called because winds generally blow from the west. Here warm tropical air meets cold polar air, and the result is storms. Regions that lie within this belt in winter but within the dry belt in summer, like the tropical wet-and-dry areas, have a rainy season and a dry season. But here, the seasons are just the opposite of those in the tropics. Western Australia is in this belt, whereas New Zealand is in the belt of the westerlies.

Mountains modify these patterns. As air blowing off the ocean is pushed up over mountains, it cools. If it is cooled enough, it will drop its moisture as rain (or snow). Therefore, the side of the high islands in the Pacific facing toward the wind is rainy, but the air reaching the other side has lost its moisture, so that side is a drier rain shadow. The Great Dividing Range of eastern Australia has this effect on the climate, increasing the dryness of the interior of the country.

RIVERS AND LAKES

Rivers are depositories of water that has fallen as precipitation and has not been used by plants or soaked into the ground. We could say they consist of surplus water that finds the lowest place to flow down to the sea. There are few major rivers in Australia and Pacific island region. The islands are too small to have rivers of any length. No rivers begin in deserts, and most of Australia is so dry that it has but one river system, the Murray-Darling. The source of the Murray-Darling system is in the Great Dividing Range, where just enough rainfall falls west of the brow of the mountains for a river to begin. In the mid-twentieth century, the government of Australia increased the water available in this system by building the Snowy Mountain Scheme. This system of reservoirs and channels in the Snowy Mountains of southeastern Australia was designed to bring more water to the eastern outback (that vast area lying just to the west of the Great Dividing Range).

Precipitation in the Great Dividing Range feeds a vital water resource for the eastern outback under the Great Artesian Basin. Rain falling on the mountains soaks into the rock layers that are tilted so that the water runs underground through water-bearing rock layers called aquifers under the eastern Outback. When wells are drilled deep enough through the overlying rock, the underground water rises in the wells, sometimes with considerable pressure.

Scattered through interior Australia are depressions where water accumulates after periods of rainfall. Because these intermittent lakes, like the Great Salt Lake in Utah, have no outlets, their waters—when there are any—are salty. The lowest place in Australia is the largest of these lakes, called Lake Eyre, in South Australia, with an elevation of 39 feet (12 meters) below sea level.

In general, the lower the average precipitation, the less reliable it is. Therefore, Australia not only has little precipitation, but it cannot count on receiving even that small amount every year. Tourists may complain if it rains the day they go to Ayers Rock (Uluṟu), but the local people rejoice. The El Niño weather phenomenon produces exceptionally dry weather over northern Australia and can bring drought to the whole country. It may not rain a single drop for years at a time. Wildfires are a distinct hazard, especially for certain trees and grasses that contain high amounts of natural plant oils. The big climatic challenge for Australians is not seasonal change, but changes over a period of years. Of course, abnormally low rainfall can occur elsewhere, too, as in the mid-1990s when a drought prompted a massive water-conservation program in Auckland, New Zealand.

PLANT AND ANIMAL LIFE

Kangaroos. Wombats. Koalas. Kiwis. Duck-billed platypus. Eucalyptus trees. The plant and animal life of this region is so unusual that it has become part of our mental image of these lands. The kangaroo and the emu (a flightless bird) appear on Australia's national coat of arms, and New Zealanders are commonly called kiwis. In the mid-1800s the botanist Alfred Russell Wallace drew a line where he saw the vegetation change from Southeast Asian forms to Australian forms. Wallace's Line passes between the Philippines and Celebes (Indonesia) and between the Indonesian islands of Bali and Sumbawa.

Geologists believe that the giant reptiles of the Mesozoic era (dinosaurs, for example) probably lived on all the continents, because the landmasses had not yet drifted so far apart that animals could not get from one to the other. Australia, like other continents, still has reptiles, including many of the world's most poisonous snakes.

By the time mammals began to evolve from reptiles and other earlier life forms, the movement of the tectonic plates and rising sea levels had created large water bodies between the continents. Different kinds of mammals developed in different parts of the world. Australia is a particularly dramatic example, with several animals that seem to be "in between" birds and reptiles, on the one hand, and mammals, on the other.

A characteristic of mammals is that their young grow for a considerable period in a womb within their mothers. This gives them a great advantage when they are born, because they are more fully mature. Furthermore, the mother feeds the young directly with milk, which is perfectly balanced nutritionally.

Mammals in Australia—marsupials such as kangaroos, koalas, wombats, and bandicoots—are somewhere in between. They bear live young, as mammals do, but their young are in no way able to live independently in the environment, even if the mothers feed them. They make their way to a special external pouch where they are protected from the elements and can nurse. There they live until they are big and strong enough to live in the outside world.

The duck-billed platypus seems to be a combination of a bird and a mammal. It has a large, leathery bill like a duck, which it uses to dig in the mud for food. It also has webbed feet, which aid in swimming, but instead of feathers, it has fur. The platypus lays eggs, but it suckles its young when they hatch. It further protects itself by keeping to waterways and their shores, and by hunting mostly at night.

Australia also has many birds, which could easily fly from neighboring New Guinea, including many brightly colored parrots and the famous laughing kookaburra. Some, like the emu, became flightless as there were no natural predators and flying takes a lot of energy, especially for a bird as large as an emu.

New Zealand is even more isolated than Australia. Life probably first reached it as floating rafts of debris riding on ocean currents. The only native animals are birds, bats, and reptiles. Like the emu of Australia, birds in New Zealand could safely live on the ground, where there was more food, and eventually some of them, like the famous kiwi, now New Zealand's national symbol, lost the ability to fly. Kiwis further protect themselves by being nocturnal.

The indigenous people of Australia and New Zealand used plants and animals for food and other needs. There were not enough of them, however, to affect the basic assortment of living things. Dogs probably arrived in Australia about 6,000 years ago. They were semidomesticated by the Aborigines, but then escaped and became wild dingoes, which prey on sheep and are a major pest. The long Dingo Fence, the longest fence in the world, was built from South Australia to northwestern Queensland in an attempt to keep the dingoes out of eastern Australia.

The arrival of European settlers changed the balance greatly, as the newcomers brought new species of plants and animals. Now the native species had a lot of competition, although the newcomers did not. Rabbits were introduced into Australia for sport in 1859, but they multiply rapidly, and there was nothing to control their population—no predators, not even disease. They quickly became a pest, as they ate grass and consumed water that livestock needed to survive. Fences were constructed and

Kiwi birds are nocturnal and cannot fly; they use their whiskers as probes to help see in the dark. The brown kiwi lives on North Island of New Zealand, whereas the Southern tokoeka kiwi, the great spotted kiwi, and the little spotted kiwi, live on South Island of New Zealand.

disease organisms introduced to try to control the rabbits, but such measures were only temporarily successful.

Australia and New Zealand have learned from these mistakes. Both countries now very carefully control organisms that enter their countries. They have strict regulations about what people may bring with them, and these are even extended to things like wooden objects and baskets. Just before an airplane lands, the flight attendants spray the cabin with pesticide so that no insects that might have flown into the plane before it took off can escape into Australia or New Zealand.

ECOSYSTEMS OF AUSTRALIA AND THE PACIFIC

Ecosystems, or communities of plants and animals that live together in a particular environment, are closely related to the climate. All living things have specific needs for nourishment and water, but they have adapted to a wide variety of environments or habitats. People have greatly changed these systems, but scientists use old documents and current plants to learn about vegetation before human settlement.

Continental Australia

Most of Australia, as we have seen, is dry, receiving 2 inches (500 millimeters) or less precipitation per year. Trees need much more precipitation than that, so forests are found only along the coasts of the continent. Other than rain forests in northeastern Queensland, the most heavily forested areas are found in southeastern Australia, Tasmania, Arnhem Land in Northern Territory, and southwestern Australia. In some places, rainfall comes at only one season, but it is sufficient for the growth of trees that are adapted to long periods of drought. Australia is understandably the continent with smallest percentage of its land forested. The name of the Nullarbor Plain in the south-central part of the country comes from Latin words meaning "no trees." For hundreds of kilometers across this very flat expanse, there are literally no trees to be seen. The world's longest straight rail line crosses the plain from Adelaide to Perth; this popular train ride takes three days.

Desert plant life consists of low shrubs or clumps of tough grass. Vegetation is widely spaced, so that each plant has a fairly large area from which to soak up available moisture. Even the sand dunes exhibit this random distribution of grass and shrub vegetation. There are a few totally barren areas, but most of them are covered with gravel or "desert pavement."

The largest plant family in Australia is the myrtle family, which includes among its more than 1,000 species more than 500 kinds of eucalyptus trees. About 100 of these grow in the arid parts of the country. Because they grow so rapidly and so well, even in dry conditions, eucalyptus trees were imported into southern California, parts of Latin America, and other arid-to-semiarid locations around the world. Eucalypts have their own oil, which is used in making cosmetics and toiletries and makes the trees very fragrant. It also helps them conserve water. They turn their leaves so that the edges are toward the sun on a hot day, so that less of the surface is subject to evaporation. This, however, makes them less useful as shade trees.

Another large tree family is the acacias (*Jacaranda*), including Australia's national flower, the wattle. Branches of the wattle tree were popular building materials among the early settlers because they could be woven together and then plastered with mud in a technique that was also widely used in Europe.

Australian marsupials have developed into many different sorts, adapted to live in all available habitats or ecological niches. Eventually, animals like koalas, the endearing subject of many ads for travel in Australia, specialized in eating the leaves of eucalyptus trees. Koalas look cuddly, but they actually have rather nasty dispositions.

Kangaroos and wallabies adapted to living in grasslands. They are shy by nature, but like white-tailed deer in the United States, they have multiplied to such numbers that they are frequently seen in more populated areas. Tragically, they are hit by cars, despite signs posted warning of kangaroo crossings.

The Islands

New Zealand's climate is much wetter than Australia's, much like the British Isles, from which the first European settlers came. The volcanic soils are rich. Consequently, most of New Zealand was originally forested. Other kinds of plants grew huge and thick, most famously, the ferns. The highest parts of the Southern Alps on South Island have alpine vegetation, similar to high mountains in Europe and North America, and the tops are snow-covered. To the east of the Southern Alps, where there is less precipitation, is an area of grassland, which is New Zealand's main sheep-raising region.

The island of New Guinea is hot and wet all year. The original vegetation is tropical rain forest with small pockets of tropical grassland, especially south of the mountains. These forests contain tropical hardwoods. Because these timber resources are valuable for furniture and other uses in rich countries, logging is reducing the amount of rain forest on New Guinea. Ecologists and conservationists are concerned that the destruction of the rain forest will lead to the extinction of other plants, which may be valuable for medicinal and other uses. Overcutting of timber also promotes erosion, as it leaves steep hillsides open to the heavy rains.

On the small islands of the Pacific, the type of ecosystem depends on the height of the island, its origin, and its size. High volcanic islands have rich volcanic soils, supporting mixed tropical rain forests, with their abundant colorful bird life. Low coral atolls tend to be sandy, and therefore less fertile. Palm trees, including coconut palms, and small grasses are the dominant plants. The lagoons may shelter tropical fish and the birds that feed on them.

Distance from other land affects the natural environment, especially the plant and animal life. Within the Australia and Pacific island region, the contrasts between continents and large islands as compared with small islands also give us the beginning of a division between subregions. Human activity increases these variations.

CHAPTER 3

Cultural History

Australia is Earth's first New World and also home of the world's oldest continuing culture. The Europeans called these people the Aborigines, from Latin words "ab" meaning "from" and "origine" meaning "beginning." By comparison, the pre-European peoples of New Zealand and the other Pacific islands are newcomers. All over the region, Europeans and other migrants from elsewhere have settled only in the last 200 years.

THE ABORIGINES OF AUSTRALIA

About 40,000 years ago—the date is still uncertain—people stood on a beach in what we know as Southeast Asia and looked south. They could see no land on the other side of the water, but there must be

This is an Aboriginal rock art painting of a nude figure, found in Australia. The Aborigines settled in Australia long before the Europeans discovered this area. The date when they first settled here is uncertain, but it is believed to be approximately 40,000 years ago.

some. Birds flew to and from something over there, and there was smoke on the horizon. Most clouds, they knew, formed over land and clouds, too, could be seen in the distance. They took to their boats and found what we now know as Australia. For the first time in human history, people had crossed a large expanse of water to discover a New World. These people were the ancestors of the Aborigines.

Aborigines lived in all parts of Australia and Tasmania before the coming of Europeans. The peoples of New Guinea are close relatives, although they developed some different ways of living. They were closely attuned to their environment, finding ways to live successfully even in dry deserts.

All Aborigines were hunters and gatherers. Men did the hunting and women the gathering, and it was the women who provided the largest share of the food. All kinds of roots, nuts, seeds, leaves, grubs, insects, and other edible material served as food. They had no sugar (except occasional wild honey) or starchy food, so they suffered almost no tooth decay. Along the coasts, where fish formed an important part of the diet, population densities were higher because fish are a more dependable food supply than land animals.

Aborigines periodically burned the land to kill weeds and bring on new growth of grasses. The fires helped to corral animals during the hunt. It was an important land-management tool among the Aborigines. Young trees did not grow up after fire as easily as did grasses, so land that was repeatedly burned supported large expanses of grassland with a few scattered trees. The first English settlers called these areas parkland. Aborigines also hunted the larger marsupials to extinction, so that present-day kinds of kangaroos and wombats are smaller than those of Australia before human habitation.

Groups of Aborigines moved from place to place in search of food. They carried very few items with them: a spear-thrower and spears, and sharpened stones for digging and for shaping wood. Their most famous tool was the boomerang, which was especially useful in the interior, where trees do not interfere. Boomerangs were made in several different shapes, only a few of them designed to return to the thrower. Some were for sport; others were for work. The end of a boomerang could also be used as a digging stick.

The kind of shelter Aborigines used depended on local conditions. In the north, they needed protection from heavy rains during the "wet" (the area's wet season). In the deserts of central Australia, they needed shelter from the sun. In the south they sheltered from cold in winter. When nights were cold, they would make several campfires and sleep between them to keep warm. They used available caves on the southeast coast for shelter. They did not weave cloth and wore little clothing.

Australians today use the term "walkabout" for an exploratory trek in the wilderness, perhaps with no fixed destination. The term comes from European observation of the movements of hunter-gatherer Aborigines. However, the Aborigines' movements were purposeful. Each group had a well-defined territory, called an estate by later Europeans, around which it moved. The center of such an estate would be a water source, or some other important or prominent resource. Each group's established estate could provide it with all necessary resources for living.

Aboriginal religious beliefs are also intimately related to the environment. They believe that before creation, there was an earth, but it was featureless and supported no living things. The world as we know it began to take shape during *tjukurpa*, which is usually translated "dreamtime," although it has nothing to do with dreams. It is a belief in a process of creation, of Earth and of humankind, and of their relationship. Dreamtime also establishes rules for behavior between humans and the environment (a very important part of geography) and for relationships between people. Their land—their particular estate—was sacred to them. Taking it away, even if it was replaced with another piece of land, destroyed their whole collective past, present, and future.

Because the Aborigines were illiterate, this information was passed from generation to generation via stories and songs. Some of it is general knowledge and has even been shared with outsiders, but some is reserved for specific groups of people and may not be revealed to anyone else. To tell somebody something is to lose control of that information. The relationships are maintained by ceremonies, some of them so sacred that only a select few people may participate or even see the ceremony. Sacred places, for example at Uluṟu (Ayers Rock), are off-limits to visitors, and no photographs are permitted.

PEOPLES OF THE ISLANDS

Like Australia's Aborigines, early settlers of the small islands came from Southeast Asia. We do not know when they moved to the islands. Stories natives tell about their ancestors' coming to the islands indicate that they probably traveled by outrigger canoe. The small islands were settled from west to east, with New Zealand last.

Melanesia

Melanesia is the island group closest to Asia and Australia. People probably came to New Guinea, New Britain, New Ireland, and the Admiralty Islands by about 30,000 years ago.

In New Guinea, near Mt. Hagen, archaeologists have found evidence of farming dating to about 9000 B.C. Thus, the people of New Guinea were among the world's first farmers. Their agricultural techniques included planting in mounds, using mulch, digging ditches, and installing bamboo irrigation channels. They grew coconut, breadfruit, yams, taro, and sweet potatoes. Like farmers in other wet tropical regions, they practiced shifting cultivation: They cleared a field, burned the under brush (which produced potash as fertilizer), and planted a crop. The field would produce for a few years, and then the weeds would be allowed to overgrow it. (The nutrients in a tropical rain forest are in the plants, not in the soil, so the soil would very quickly lose its fertility. The hot sun would also eventually bake the soil into hard clay.) A new field would be cleared and the process started anew. The old field would be left unplanted, so that the weeds would grow, die, and decay, restoring the land for the next crop.

New Guinea supported many groups who lived this way, each in a fairly small area. Nevertheless, groups traded with each other. Trade networks covered a wide area, leading to very different cultures on the island as different groups specialized in different kinds of crafts. Through trade, groups obtained such goods as clay pots, stone tools, and ceremonial goods and practices. People who were especially good at trade became leaders in the groups; otherwise, everyone was equal. Some trade exchanges involved long sea voyages among the smaller islands to the northeast of New Guinea.

Micronesia

Micronesia has a few high, volcanic islands. On these high islands, such as Yap, Pohnpei, Chuuk, Guam, and Palau, early people grew crops and fished in the surrounding waters.

Most of the islands are atolls and therefore lack abundant fresh water. Survival on such islands, therefore, depended upon finding sufficient water. These islands have few streams, and the coral soils do not retain water well, so people had to rely on brackish water from wells. Few crops could be grown in these conditions. Coconut palms resist saltwater, and breadfruit can be grown and stored in pits. Swamp taro was planted in natural depressions, or in dug pits where a freshwater "lens" sits on top of saltwater. It must be heavily mulched to retain moisture, but it grows year-round and can withstand drought. Consequently, it was a very valuable foodstuff, supplemented by fish from the sea and the lagoons.

People relied on a whole network of islands, not just the one on which they lived. They became excellent seafarers, especially those on small islands. (Residents of larger islands were regarded as landlubbers.) Their ship was the outrigger canoe, sailed by a navigator and four to six seamen. Becoming a navigator required extensive study and gave one great status in the society. The Micronesians made elaborate maps, using cane to indicate currents and other features and shells to lo-

Kaibula men paddle an outrigger canoe near Trobriand Island, New Guinea. The outrigger canoe was a vital means of transportation, communication, and trade. An outrigger canoe navigator (standing) was required to study extensively to achieve the position and was awarded great status among his people.

cate islands. They sailed long distances out of sight of land, using stars to navigate and naming directions according to the islands they faced. These voyages sustained trade and complex relationships between groups. Status in the very hierarchical society depended on one's success in such trade as well as ownership of land.

Polynesia

Most of Polynesia consists of high, volcanic islands that have a rainy side and a dry side. Early Polynesians lived by farming and fishing. Settlements tended to be near the shore, whereas gardens and plantations were located farther inland. There they raised taro, yams, and kumara, a variety of sweet potatoes. Sweet potatoes are native to the Andes of South America; how the Polynesians obtained them is a mystery. In 1947, a Norwegian anthropologist and explorer named Thor Heyerdahl sailed a raft built of reeds called *Kon-Tiki* from Peru to the Tuamotu Islands to demonstrate that early Polynesians could have come from South America. Most other evidence points to their coming from Asia, but quite possibly there were contacts between South America and Polynesia before the European voyages of exploration.

Polynesians placed great emphasis on rank. Chiefs were the closest to the gods and were called "father of the people." Their persons were sacred, or *tapu* (the origin of our word *taboo*), and they were thought to be endowed with divine power. They were both political and religious leaders and had power of life and death over their subjects. Some of them, such as Kamehameha I in Hawaii, established small states as they expanded their authority over thousands of people.

One of the last groups of islands to be settled was New Zealand, far from any other land. Archaeologists believe that the Maori may have come to New Zealand as early as A.D. 700, but certainly by A.D. 1000. The settlers probably began coming in large numbers in the 1300s when a fleet of 12 large canoes arrived from the Society Islands in what is today French Polynesia. The new settlers were probably escaping food shortages on their native islands. Although there is no archaeological evidence of these canoes, they are important to Maori people today, who trace their ancestry to these canoe-loads of settlers.

The Maori brought food crops, including taro, yams, and kumara; they also brought rats and dogs. New Zealand was a rich land. Fish and a flightless bird called the moa provided ample protein. Not only was the moa flightless, but it also was tame, as it had no natural enemies before people settled the region. Sadly, it was soon hunted to extinction.

Growing familiar crops provided some challenges. New Zealand is colder than the tropical islands. Kumara would not grow year-round. The people quickly discovered, however, that they could dig up the tubers in the autumn, store them in pits in the earth, and plant them again in the spring.

Because the mulberry tree, which they had used to make *tapa*, or bark cloth, would not grow in New Zealand, the settlers learned to weave native flax for cloth, ropes, and baskets. The abundance of trees in New Zealand made possible large canoes, and woodcarving became an established craft. The Maori also built wooden homes and meeting halls called *marae*. They developed one of the most sophisticated societies in the pre-European world, with an elaborate social structure and wide trading networks.

When the climate cooled beginning in the 1300s, familiar crops would not grow. People began eating more shellfish, which contained small amounts of sand, and fern roots. Both were hard on their teeth, and by the time people reached their twenties, their teeth had worn away. Only when contact with the Americas in the 1500s brought the potato to New Zealand was there again a reliable food supply.

Like other Polynesians, the Maori had a very hierarchical society. They lived in villages of 500 or more households. Tribal affiliation was (and is) important to the Maori, as it determines who may marry whom—and even who fights whom. The village was centered around the marae, where guests were welcomed, once they had demonstrated their goodwill and friendship. This traditional welcome survives today in communities, even university campuses, that have a marae and hold a traditional welcome ceremony, for example, at the beginning of an academic conference.

As intertribal warfare increased because of greater scarcity of food, many of the villages, called *pa*, were established on volcanic hills, where terracing provided more flat land for building. The pa were also fortified with palisades and ditches. The largest and most imposing pa is Maungakiekie, or One Tree Hill, in Auckland, with several volcanic craters, many terraces, and remains of such features as food-storage pits.

EUROPEAN EXPLORATION AND SETTLEMENT

Australia and the Pacific Ocean, located on the other side of the world from Europe, was the last inhabited land to become known to Europeans. Since ancient times, Europeans reasoned that there must be land in the southern part of the world to "balance" the land masses that they knew in the north, but they had no proof.

European Exploration

The first European explorers, in the 1500s, were the Spanish. In the 1600s and early 1700s, the Dutch arrived. Among other things, Spanish and Dutch explorers contributed to the region a long list of place names.

Interest in Australia and the Pacific emerged again in the 1700s as competition to find new lands increased between the French and the British. The British captain James Cook finally confirmed that Australia was the great southern continent. While much of it seemed unfit for European settlement—a great disappointment—the southeast coast, which he called New South Wales, would support "civilization." Not that it had products of great value, but at least people could gain a living there. On his three major voyages, Captain Cook also visited Tahiti, New Zealand, and Hawaii, as well as places in the far northern Pacific and the waters off Antarctica.

Captain Cook's long voyages benefited from a major advance in studies in nutrition. Not only were the small ships of the day unable to carry large quantities of supplies, but fresh food spoiled on the long voyages. Sailors' diets seriously lacked Vitamin C, found most abundantly in citrus fruits like oranges, lemons, and limes, and as a result they came down with scurvy. The danger of scurvy cooled the desire of many explorers to attempt long trans-Pacific voyages. Then, in 1753, Dr. James Lind found the cure: a daily dose of citrus-fruit juice. British sea captains began to adopt this regimen, and to this day, British sailors are nicknamed "limeys." Cook, always mindful of his crews' welfare, did not lose a single sailor to scurvy on his expeditions.

Many of the explorers visited the islands, in part to purchase supplies for their ships. When Cook visited the Tonga Islands in 1773, he also released some of the livestock he carried on board and planted seeds on the islands. The islands were soon home to European pigs (which were larger than the native ones), cattle, and sheep. Among the plants were citrus trees, vines, papaya, pineapple, root vegetables, and cereal grains. When expeditions returned, they could purchase supplies of these foods. The islanders were especially eager to obtain goods like the cloth and iron nails that the Europeans brought.

Missionaries followed the traders and explorers. An unfortunate unintended consequence of the missions was the spread of disease. Like the native peoples of the Americas, the isolated populations of the Pacific islands had no immunity to European diseases such as smallpox, and especially measles and influenza. Consequently, disease spread rapidly, killing large numbers of people. In traditional societies, the family structure would keep groups of people somewhat separated from each other. The missionaries, however, wanted people from all families to worship together. This brought them into contact with one another, which helped to spread disease.

Australia: The First Penal Continent

Beginning in the 1730s, the British government had solved the problem of its overcrowded prisons by shipping prisoners, primarily debtors, to North America. Georgia was founded as a prison colony. However, after the colonies won their independence from Britain in 1783, this outlet for British prisoners was no longer available. The British finally decided to send convicts to what Captain Cook had called New South Wales. It appeared to offer little promise as a place to live or to find resources to create great wealth. Therefore, it seemed to be a perfect place to send prisoners. Furthermore, it was so far away that once transported there, the settlers could do little harm.

On May 13, 1787, the First Fleet of eleven ships with 750 convicts—accompanied by Captain Arthur Phillip as governor and 250 military guards—set sail from Portsmouth, England. Never had such a long voyage been undertaken by such a large group of people. The convicts knew nothing about the place to which they were going; just that it was very far away. They arrived in Australia in January 1788.

At first, the settlers lived in tents. Gradually, they built houses by erecting upright posts and then filling in the spaces with woven flexible small branches of a local mimosa tree. Then they covered the walls with mud. This kind of construction, which was common in England at the time, was called wattle and daub. To this day, Australians call that kind of mimosa tree the "wattle." The heavy rains washed the mud out of the cracks, however, leaving the houses leaky and drafty. The available reeds from the wetlands also proved to be very poor thatch for roofs. As the settlers explored the area more thoroughly, they found some suitable clay for making bricks, but the only lime to make the mortar between the bricks was seashells. Hauling them was difficult, and suitable mortar remained in short supply. The bricks proved to be poor quality, especially in heavy rain. None of the buildings survive to the present.

By the time Britain stopped sending convicts in 1868, Australia's beginnings as a gigantic jail for convicts and their guards had a lasting effect on the society that developed there. Some of the prisoners had been convicted for what we would consider very minor infractions; others had committed more serious crimes, some of them more than once. A very few were political prisoners. In the early 1800s, Irish rebels swelled the number of prisoners. The Irish were the first white minority in Australia and suffered much discrimination. They were also the beginning of the Roman Catholic community in Australia.

Once they served their sentences (which sometimes was shortened), the convicts could own land and settle down to build new lives. For many years, Australians tried to forget their origins as a penal colony, and no one proudly announced convict ancestry. They wanted to forge a new kind of country—but from what? Their school system was modeled on that of Britain, and children learned about British geography and history. Australia seemed like a blank slate, if they could not talk about its beginnings as a jail. Late in the twentieth century, especially as they approached the bicentennial of the First Fleet, they began to look back with more pride. A group of convicts, many with few or no skills, had formed a vibrant, prosperous society. The country was democratic, and it established programs to take care of children, the elderly, the sick, and the disabled. Concern for these kinds of issues had come from the settlers' difficult beginning there.

Free settlers joined the migration to Australia, especially after gold was discovered there in the 1850s. The first discovery was near Bathurst, in New South Wales, followed soon after by several strikes in the state of Victoria. The biggest gold deposits were in Western Australia, especially around Kalgoorlie, which proved to be possibly the world's richest. The gold strike turned Western Australia from the poorest state to the richest. Great wealth and many immigrants from all over the world came as a result of the discoveries.

Its beginnings as a penal colony and the gold rushes also gave Australia the strong quality of "mateship," meaning comradeship or looking out for one's friends. People greet each other as "mate," but it also means a deep level of devotion, loyalty, affection, and mutual dependence. Mateship also involves sympathy for the underdog. Equality and a healthy disregard for authority and ideology are important traits. The right to a "fair go" means that the arbitrary exercise of power and privilege by the strong over the weak is unacceptable.

Settlement of New Zealand

New Zealand was settled by volunteers; there were no organized expeditions to plant colonies. In 1792, a boat from Sydney, Australia, left a group of seal hunters on South Island, and about the same time whalers began hunting in New Zealand waters.

After 1800, whalers from Britain, the United States, and France often stopped at the Bay of Islands to resupply and repair their vessels and to trade with the Maori. Seal and whale hunting ships began leaving small groups of crew members to set up a rough camp at a promising spot to hunt whales and seals and to provide skins and oil for their ships on return. Although the lifestyles there were extremely primitive, some of these little camps were remarkably successful. Later they added flax and timber to the products they could sell.

In the early 1800s, immigrants had more contact with the Maori, who helped cut timber and joined the crews of whaling vessels. New plants, especially the potato, and new animals such as European pigs, were introduced to New Zealand and found a ready market among the ships that called. Eventually, the most important trading community developed at Kororareka (now called Russell) in the Bay of Islands, in northern North Island. The Maori were especially eager to obtain metal nails, which they could make into all kinds of tools. They also liked red paint or cloth; red was their favorite color and was used to mark sacred objects. Besides traders, the community included missionaries, a doctor, a sawyer, a blacksmith, and other tradespeople, who prospered by providing repair services to ships.

Smaller Pacific Islands

Like New Zealand, the islands of Polynesia, Melanesia, and Micronesia were ports of call for whalehunting, sealhunting, and trading ships. These voyages became much more frequent in the 1800s. Their reports to Europe, however, made the islands seem very unappealing for settlement. What attracted Europeans to Fiji was sandalwood, a fragrant wood that was highly prized in Asia. Most of the traders came from Australia, and they stripped Fiji of its sandalwood forests within 10 years of their arrival in 1804. The Melanesians tolerated them because they traded iron axes and other desirable items. When the forests of Fiji were cut, the traders moved on to New Caledonia and then to the New Hebrides.

Britain was not the only country to send prisoners to colonies as far from home as possible. The French took New Caledonia in 1854 with the same purpose in mind. From 1864 to 1897, France sent more than 22,000 convicts to the remote island. Like those in Australia, prisoners worked on government projects, but also in forestry, mining, and farming. As plantations and mines grew, however, there were not enough convicts, and the French supplemented their labor with indentured workers from elsewhere, especially the New Hebrides and the Solomon Islands. Political prisoners began arriving in 1872. They included professional people like doctors and lawyers who were strong believers in equality and public social services.

Europeans began seizing people from Melanesia, especially the New Hebrides and the Solomons, for work on the sugar plantations of Queensland, Australia. Aborigines were regarded as subhuman and therefore as unsuitable labor. They could also slip away to rejoin their families, and many died of European diseases to which they had no immunity. Some Melanesians were brought as indentured servants with contracts specifying their pay, but many were captured and brought as virtual slaves by what was called "blackbirding." The federal government of Australia outlawed the practice in 1904, and the Melanesians were transported back to the islands and simply dumped.

Pitcairn Island in Polynesia has an entirely different history. In 1787, the HMS *Bounty* set sail from England under Captain William Bligh on the first commercial venture of the British in the South Pacific. Bligh purchased breadfruit trees in Tahiti to take to Jamaica, to provide food for slaves. Three weeks after leaving Tahiti, the master's mate, Fletcher Christian, mutinied and seized the ship. Bligh and 18 of the crew were set adrift in the *Bounty*'s longboat.

Christian and the remaining crew settled on Pitcairn Island. So isolated is Pitcairn by distance, currents, and reefs that the British government did not find the community until 1808. Bligh and the rest in the longboat, remarkably, made their way across the Pacific to Batavia (present-day Jakarta,

Indonesia) in the Dutch East Indies and from there back to England on a Dutch ship.

Once Britain took control of Fiji in 1874 and began to establish plantations there, the British found a source of workers in India, which it also ruled. Once the South Asians had completed their indenture, they were encouraged to remain in Fiji, and they remain a prominent part of the population today.

When European officials came to New Guinea, they received supplies in huge wooden crates. The people of New Guinea thought that the crates gave the Europeans their power. In the "cargo cults" that resulted, they carried crates around to obtain this power and built ports for the ships that would bring the cargo. Later, they added airplanes to the transportation modes and built landing strips. The cargo cults are a unique window on the effect of European settlement on the indigenous populations.

NEW IMMIGRANTS TO "DOWN UNDER"

Europeans were not the only settlers in Australia and New Zealand in the 1800s. People from many lands came to Australia to look for gold, and New Zealand attracted people from Asia along with the Europeans. In the early 1900s, however, both countries began to restrict non-British immigration. "White Australia" was the policy, and New Zealand's was similar.

After World War II, Australians began to realize that Britain would not supply enough immigrants to fill up their empty land. The country's policy of "Populate or Perish" meant they would have to allow immigration from lands that, like England in the late 1700s, were overcrowded. First came refugees from Adolph Hitler's persecution of Jews and others, the destruction of World War II, and the imposition of Communism in Eastern Europe. Ever-increasing numbers of Italians, Greeks, Hungarians, Yugoslavs, and East Germans arrived. In the 1970s the infamous White Australia policy ended, and Australia became a land of opportunity for South, Southeast, and East Asians. Chinatowns appeared in the larger cities, and life became much more multicultural and varied, with a wide diversity of ethnic restaurants and popular culture. New Zealand, too, began to attract more migrants from Asia with similar results.

From earliest pre-history, different groups have settled the various parts of Australia and the Pacific, and they have formed different societies and relationships to each other. These distinctions continue to make their mark on the region today.

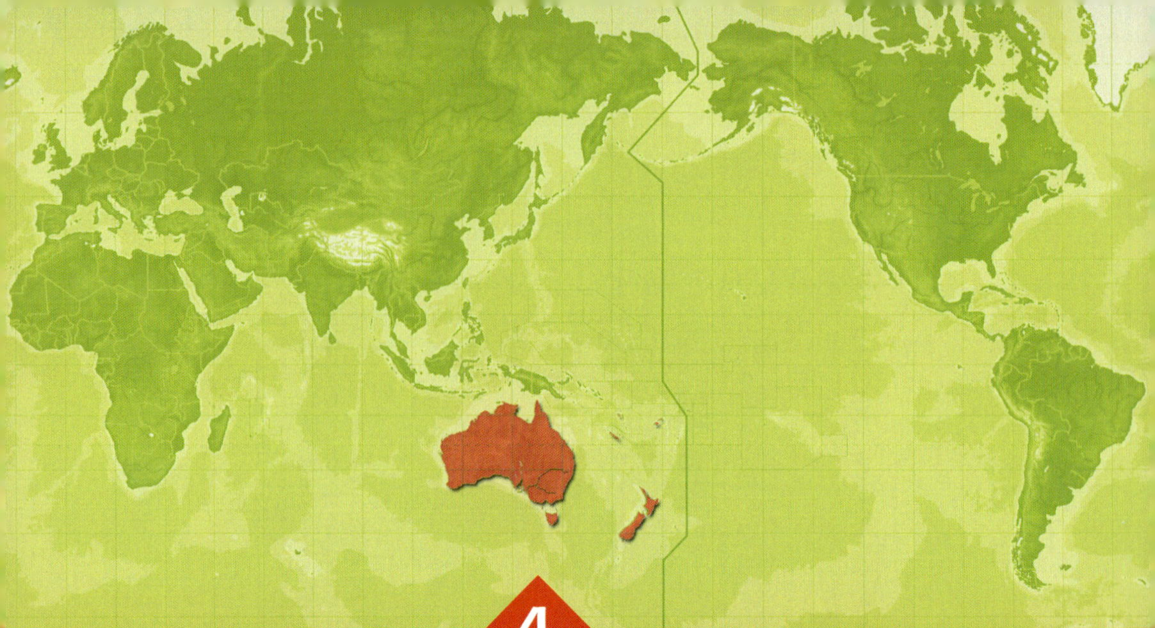

CHAPTER 4

People and Culture

Australia, New Zealand, and the Pacific islands today include regions of very different population characteristics and cultural patterns. Australia and New Zealand were settled by large numbers of Europeans who came to live permanently and dominated the people they found. In the Pacific islands, fewer Europeans came to live, and the population today comprises primarily descendents of those who lived there before the days of European expansion. Their lives today, however, are quite different from those of their ancestors, who greeted European explorers and traders.

POPULATION

None of the countries in this region has a very large population. Even huge Australia, which is both a country and a continent, has relatively

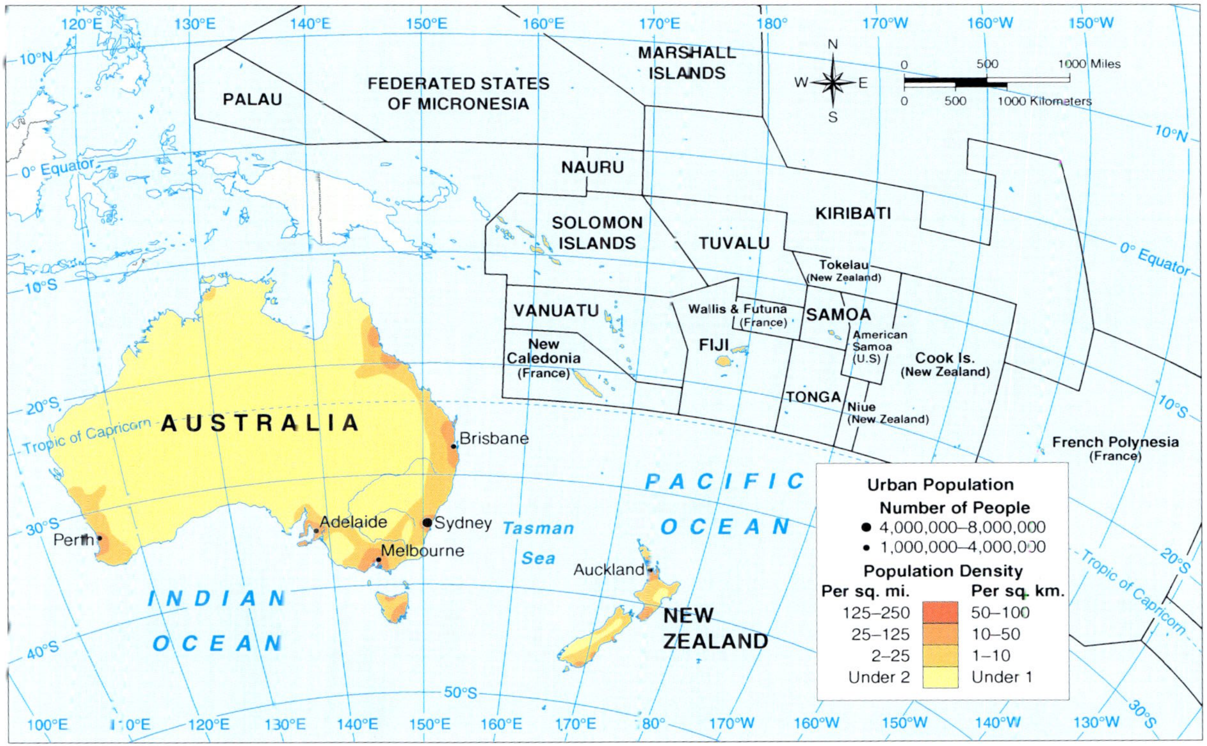

Australia has a relatively small population for its size. Vast areas of Australia are only sparsely inhabited because of the harsh desert climate. Most of the population can be found in cities along the southeast coast. New Zealand and the Pacific islands have small, but growing populations.

very few people. Despite immigration, the populations of Australia and New Zealand are growing slowly. Those of the islands, small to begin with, are growing at a faster rate.

Australia and New Zealand

Australia and New Zealand are wealthy countries where most people are highly educated and hold nonagricultural jobs. Farmers sell their produce on the market and buy what they need, including most of their food, in stores.

Characteristics of the population match in these two countries. Families are small. In Australia and New Zealand, women on average give birth to fewer than two children each. That means that, if there were no immigration, the population of Australia and New Zealand would decline, because families on average do not have enough children to replace the parent generation. Because some children die before they grow up, the average number of children per woman must exceed 2.1 if a population is to grow. Most people decide how many children to have for personal reasons, such as how many they can afford and wish to raise. Few people, in making this important decision, consider the impact on the country's population as a whole. The decision does make a difference, however. Countries with smaller families do not need to provide as many schools. Fewer people each year enter the labor force and need jobs. Only 20 percent of Australia's population and 22 percent of New Zealand's are under 15 years of age, the standard definition of childhood.

Both countries provide good levels of nutrition and health care for their people, so people live long lives. In Australia the average life span is 80 years, and in New Zealand it is 78. Therefore, a relatively high percentage of the population in both countries is retired: 13 percent of Australians and 12 percent of New Zealanders are over 65. Therefore, both countries, rather than having to provide schools and day-care centers and entry-level jobs, are faced with the challenge of supporting retired citizens, including housing, recreation, and health care.

Countries in which fewer babies are born and thus families are small tend to increase their populations slowly. Growth in Australia and New Zealand is less than 1 percent per year. Excluding immigration, it will take both countries more than 70 years to double their populations. Australia's population now is about 20 million. If present trends continue, by 2025 it will be about 25 million, and by 2050, not quite 30 million. New Zealand's population today is about 4 million. By 2025 it will be not quite 5 million, and by 2050 it will be just over that.

Small Island Countries

The small island countries present a very different picture. There are few opportunities there for employment at nonagricultural occupations, and the economies of most islands are very poorly developed. Large families are the norm. For example, in the Marshall Islands of Micronesia, the average number of children per woman is almost six, in the Solomon Islands it is almost five, and in Vanuatu, Federated States of Micronesia, and Papua New Guinea it is more than four. Not surprisingly, these countries have a very high percentage of children—40 percent or more—in their populations. At the same time, people there do not live as long. The average life span is less than 70 years, and in Papua New Guinea, it is less than 60. The percentage of elderly is less than 5 percent.

There are many consequences to this pattern. First of all, these countries need many schools. They also need jobs for the young people when they finish school. In Fiji, for example, about 2,500 young people graduate from school each year, but there are nowhere near as many jobs that require an education. Many of the young people graduate from high school only to find jobs such as serving coffee at a tourist resort.

Although these countries may not be faced with the challenge of supporting as many elderly citizens for as many years as do Australia and New Zealand, their society lacks their elders' knowledge. Furthermore, if people die young, they have not had a chance to enjoy a productive career or to save for their old age, although they required nurturing and an education when they were growing up. People who live longer can save for their retirement, and they have also enjoyed long careers, contributing to society. In many of the island countries, babies may die before they reach one year of age. In Papua New Guinea, for example, 60 babies die for every 1,000 born; in Australia and New Zealand, only about five do. This high rate of death is one reason why people have many children, to ensure that some will live to reach adulthood.

Despite early deaths, the populations of these countries are growing fast. All of them are increasing at least one percent a year, and the Marshall Islands and Solomon Islands are growing at over 3 percent per year. That may not sound like much, but the population of Marshall Islands will double in less than 20 years.

SETTLEMENT PATTERNS

In most of these countries, population is unevenly distributed. Some parts of the country are more attractive for settlement and have more resources than others.

Australia is a particularly dramatic example. Most of its 20 million people live in the southeast, in a belt extending from Adelaide in South Australia around the coast to Brisbane in Queensland. Australians call this region the "Boomerang Coast" because of its shape. The area around Perth is another settled part of the country, separated by nearly 1,500 miles (2,400 kilometers) of outback (Australian desert). In the far north, Darwin is an important town on the coast of the Arafura Sea. About 80 percent of Australians live in cities.

The middle of Australia, the outback, is dry, covered with scrub vegetation or desert. A few settlements dot this empty land, such as Alice Springs and Kalgoorlie, where water and mineral deposits attracted settlers. Since the days when early explorers died in the outback, distance has always been a major

Here is the famous Sydney Opera House, Sydney, Australia. Approximately 80 percent of Australia's population live in the cities. Most of these are in the Southeast, where settlement was more attractive.

challenge. Today, with modern technology, the people can communicate with the rest of the world, but in the early days, living in the outback was a lonely existence. Until 2004, the north-south railroad through the middle of the country from Adelaide ended at Alice Springs. In January 2004 the extension north to Darwin finally opened. Alice Springs itself began as a station on a long telegraph line to connect Adelaide to Darwin and then to Singapore (also a British colony) and the world at large.

Settlement in New Zealand also hugs the coastline, but for a different reason. The middle of the islands, especially South Island, is mountainous. It is a favorite vacation spot because of its scenery, hiking, camping, and skiing, but few people live in the mountains. About 78 percent of New Zealanders live in cities. Over all, New Zealand is somewhat more densely populated than Australia, with 38 persons per square mile (15 per square kilometer) to Australia's seven per square mile (three per square kilometer).

ETHNIC AND CULTURAL GROUPS

As the last chapter showed, the people of all these countries are descendents of pre-European peoples and European settlers. More recent immigrants have added to the mix. The relationships among all these groups vary greatly from one part of the region to another.

Australia

When Europeans began to settle Australia, there were perhaps 300,000 to 500,000 Aborigines throughout the entire continent. Nobody knows for sure how many there were. Very quickly, their numbers declined to about 60,000 by 1930. They had been completely wiped out from Tasmania by 1835. However, descendents of Aboriginal Tasmanian (Palawa) mothers and European fathers retained the Aboriginal culture. They remain an important force. For example, in 1981, their protests prevented the construction of a dam that would have flooded traditionally sacred sites.

Europeans expected the Aborigines simply to disappear from the area, to go do their hunting and gathering elsewhere. Because the Aborigines were not farmers and did not own land outright as Europeans did, the settlers believed that no one owned the land. They simply took it for their own uses, and they reinforced their land ownership with fences.

The Aborigines' ties to the land went far deeper than just hunting the animals and gathering plant food. One piece of land was not just as good as another, for the Aborigines' whole way of life, including their belief system, was tied to a particular place. As Europeans migrated inland, they disrupted the estates in which the Aborigines traveled. In doing so, they tore from the Aborigines their whole identity and sense of place. They also destroyed the resources that sustained the Aborigine peoples.

The most devastating European import, however, was disease. The Aborigines had had almost no contact with the rest of the world for thousands of years. They had no immunity to common European diseases like measles, smallpox, and influenza. Europeans also killed Aborigines in war, or even just for sport.

The Europeans considered the Aboriginal culture, which did not include farming, wearing clothes, or Christianity, to be "inferior" to that of the Europeans. In the late 1800s and early 1900s, the European settlers tried to force European culture on the Aborigines by taking Aboriginal children and placing them in boarding schools far from their homes. The children were not permitted to speak their native language or have contact with their families. The project failed miserably and destroyed the children's cultural roots.

Late in the twentieth century, attitudes began to change. In 1976, the government passed the Northern Territory Aboriginal Land Rights Act. This legislation finally began to reverse the belief that nobody had lived in Australia before 1788. Large tracts of land in Northern Territory were turned over to Aboriginal ownership, although the act excluded land in towns or otherwise owned by anyone else. The only exception was Uluṟu-Kata Tjuta National Park (Ayers Rock and the Olgas), which was already a conservation area and was leased back to Australia's National Park Service. Today, it is managed by a board made up of both white Australians and Aborigines. In other states, too, land has been turned over to Aboriginal ownership, and non-Aboriginals must obtain special permits even to drive through these reservations. In the far north, the reservations include tropical rain forests, but most reservations are in the driest parts of the country.

Before the arrival of Europeans, Aborigines spoke about 250 different languages and about 700 dialects. Aborigines in the outback still speak at least 100 of these, each with several dialects. The language in the area of Uluṟu-Kata Tjuta is Pitjantjatjara, with only two vowels and 17 consonants. A phonetic transcription, developed by white Australians, is used on some of the signs in the national park. Very few non-Aborigines speak Aboriginal languages.

Aborigines long ago developed arts, including music, painting (on rocks and bark), and carving. They invented a long wind instrument called the djeridoo, which sounds like a deep-pitched flute, to accompany their singing. Non-Aborigines have become interested in these arts, and Aboriginal artists now sell their works to white Australians and to visitors.

The Aborigines of Australia continue to suffer more poverty, lower rates of health and well-being, and lower education levels than other Australians. Making up about one percent of the population, their average life span is only 50 to 60 years, and three to four times as many Aborigine babies as non-Aborigine babies die before their first birthday. Many more Aborigine children suffer from disease, and fewer attend school. They are objects of discrimination, and most live geographically and economically on the margins of the country. Australia is still struggling with the challenge of improving their lives and strengthening their cultural roots.

New Zealand

The first European settlements in New Zealand were small trading centers, supplying passing ships. The native Maori tolerated their presence because from these settlers they could obtain much-valued European goods in return for food and wood. Furthermore, they quickly understood the strength of European guns. Nearby Maori chiefs acquired guns of their own, giving them power to expand the land under their control. Possession of other European goods also increased their status in the very class-conscious society.

Missionaries began arriving in 1814, first from the Church Missionary Society (Church of England) and then the Methodists and Catholics. They taught not only religion but also new farming methods and reading and writing. Being able to read and write gave those who had the skills greater status.

These new ideas also disrupted the traditional Maori culture, however. Not only did Europeans possess iron tools and

European missionaries began arriving in Fiji in the early 1800s. Because of their activity, a little more than one-third of the people of Fiji are Methodist.

guns, but they also seemed to be able to cure at least some cases of the diseases they had brought, which were decimating the population. The missionaries undertook to mediate the tribal wars. Their God, too, seemed to have more power than the Maori gods. Many Maori converted to Christianity.

The Treaty of Waitangi did not end warfare between Europeans and the Maori, and this warfare continued until 1881. Meanwhile the Europeans, known as *Pakeha* in Maori, continued to invade the countryside, taking Maori land for their own use. Maori died in wars and from diseases, and their population had declined to about 45,000 by 1900. Holding low-status jobs as laborers, they suffered from poverty. Much of their land was far from the economic centers of the country.

In the twentieth century, their resilience became more evident. Inspired by the American Civil Rights movement, they began to apply political pressure for equality and for the return of their lands. The landownership question remains complicated, as, of course, other people are living on those lands now and regard them as their property.

Meanwhile, Maori began to rediscover their traditional arts and language. New Zealand is the only country that is both dominated by the descendents of European settlers and officially bilingual in the settlers' and the native languages: Maori and English. The official name of the country is Aotearoa/New Zealand. Books are printed in Maori or both languages (including the prayer book of the Anglican Church of New Zealand). Many Pakeha can speak at least a little Maori. Maori art and carving are very popular with New Zealanders and visitors alike. Most Maori who practice a religion are Christian, but groups of Maori also celebrate traditional religious practices. About 10 percent of New Zealanders are Maori, and most live on North Island.

European Australians and New Zealanders

Descendents of European settlers, especially the British, form the largest proportion of the populations of Australia (92 percent) and New Zealand (about 75 percent). Not surprisingly, the dominant language in both countries is English. After their long geographical separation from Britain, however, Australians in particular have developed their own accent and vocabulary. For example, the bush is an area outside a city, and bush tucker is outback food. Other words entered Australian English from Aboriginal languages; these include kangaroo, wallaby, and dingo.

The same dominance of Europeans gives both countries their Christian majorities. Dating from the Irish convicts in the First Fleet and increased with later immigration from Eastern and Southern Europe, Australia has more Catholics (26 percent) than New Zealand (15 percent). Both countries are about one-quarter Anglican. In Australia, other Protestant denominations have combined to form the Uniting Church of Australia, while in New Zealand they remain separate. Both countries enjoy complete religious freedom and today have added various New Age groups to the mix. In both, however, religious membership is declining, as people's lives revolve around other interests.

As we have seen, in the late twentieth century, both Australia and New Zealand began accepting non-European immigrants to their countries. In both countries, the number of immigrants (those moving in) minus the number of emigrants (those departing) is about 4 per 1,000 residents. Australia has a somewhat more diverse population than New Zealand. Both countries have special relationships with the Pacific islands, allowing residents of those countries to come and go very much like citizens. Pacific islanders attend universities and have special rights to move to Australia and New Zealand to work. Along with Asians they have brought new customs, foods, restaurants, and religious landscapes. Asians make up about 7 percent of the population of both countries. Pacific islanders make up almost 4 percent of New Zealand's population, and European immigrants about 5 percent.

However, in both countries, immigration remains controversial. Both countries have small populations that are growing slowly. They have turned to immigration as a way to increase their populations and to bring needed skills. But some residents of both countries are concerned that too many immigrants will take jobs from people who are already there. Immigrants may cause stress on social services, health care, and education. They may also bring new cultural traits—ways of thinking and doing—that would change these countries. Especially in times of high unemployment, groups opposed to immigration press their governments to limit the number of newcomers.

Pacific Islands

Compared with the situation in Australia and New Zealand, in colonial times, few Europeans moved to the Pacific islands. Most of those who did were government officials or investors who wanted to start plantations, open mines, or log forests to send tropical products back to Europe. Thus, they came with the idea of being the owners and managers and having the local people work for them. Most of the groups of islands are now independent, but much of the economy remains foreign-owned.

Today, native Polynesians, Melanesians, and Micronesians make up the majority of the people on all the islands. There are also some non-Europeans, especially Chinese, who have come to the islands seeking work.

Fiji still has a significant number of South Asians (44 percent of the population), dating from the times when the British brought them to work on sugarcane plantations. Prohibited from owning land, many of the Asians have opened small stores, restaurants, and Internet cafes. Their religions are also visible in the landscape, as 38 percent of Fijians are Hindu and 8 percent are Muslim. Their proportion of the population is declining, as many move away from Fiji to seek opportunities elsewhere.

Fiji lies on the boundary between Melanesia and Polynesia. A little more than half of the population of Fiji is native Fijian, with a mixture of Melanesian and Polynesian ancestry. Missionaries brought Christianity to Fiji—first the Methodists, who now account for 37 percent of the population.

Melanesia, especially Papua New Guinea, still displays great language diversity. As people of different languages, including Europeans, needed to communicate with each other, they developed simple speech using words from both languages. Such languages are called *pidgin,* and pidgin languages have become standardized and have been widely adopted in Melanesia. Tok pisin is the language in Papua New Guinea, Pijin in the Solomon Islands, and Bislama in Vanuatu. They are similar enough that they give a sense of unity to all of Melanesia.

In many of the Pacific islands, the old colonial languages of English and French are widely used because people whose native languages are different have learned these languages in school. English is the official language in Fiji, for example, with Fijian and Hindustani (a language from India) also used.

Characteristics of the various cultural groups show the divisions within Australia and the Pacific islands between the populations of wealthy countries and those of the less developed world, who have lower standards of living. These differences are also reflected in political systems and in ways of earning a living.

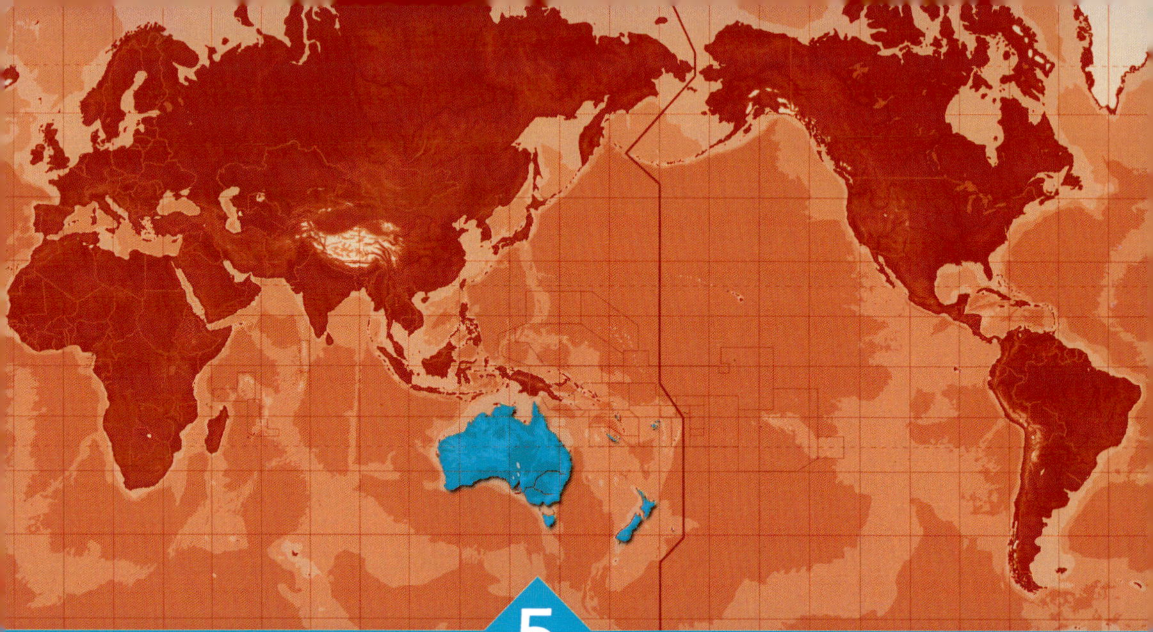

CHAPTER 5

Geopolitics

The political role of Australia and the Pacific in the world is related to the region's location. This role has changed over the years, as the world's political situation has changed. Likewise, the countries in this area of the world have developed different internal forms of government and political structures.

COLONIAL RULE AND INDEPENDENCE

As we have seen, Europeans set up colonies in all parts of this region. Many areas became colonies of one power just to keep another power from taking over. A few were governed jointly by more than one power. Britain and France ruled most of the region.

Australia and New Zealand

As was discussed earlier, at first the British used Australia as a penal colony, but later settlers came voluntarily. South Australia was never a prison colony. By the late nineteenth century, Australia comprised six separate colonies, five on the continent and one adjacent island: Queensland, New South Wales, Victoria, South Australia, Western Australia, and the island colony of Tasmania. Each colony had its own government, laws, customs, and duties—and even different railroad gauges (the space between the rails). Premiers of the colonies met from time to time to discuss matters of common concern, but mutual distrust and petty jealousies kept them separated.

Finally in 1891, there appeared to be a threat of invasion by China. Meetings began in Sydney to form a confederation, under the leadership of Sir Henry Parkes, Australia's "Father of the Confederation." In 1898, a constitution was presented to the individual colonies for a vote. It provided for a federation under the British monarch, who would be represented by a governor-general. Internal matters would be decided by a Parliament. In 1901, the confederation went into effect. Australia became the second dominion in the British Empire, after Canada (which had gained dominion status in 1867).

The British Crown took over New Zealand as a colony in 1840. William Hobson (representing the British government) signed the Treaty of Waitangi with the Maori chiefs. The Maori agreed to British sovereignty and were allowed to keep their land. The capital was located at present-day Auckland, which was halfway between the settlements at the Bay of Islands and a new settlement at Port Nicholson (present-day Wellington).

In 1852, New Zealand acquired a new constitution. Property qualifications for voting effectively excluded the Maori because they did not own land individually. Almost all of the European settlers, however, were able to vote. In 1893, New Zealand became the first country in the world to grant women the right to vote. By a 1907 act of the British Parliament, New Zealand became a dominion within the British Empire.

This is the house where the Treaty of Waitangi was signed, Waitangi, North Island, New Zealand. In 1840, the Maori signed a treaty with the British which agreed to British sovereignty over New Zealand and allowed the Maori to keep their land.

Pacific Islands

Beginning in the late eighteenth century, the British and the French seized most of the small islands of the Pacific in a mad scramble for territory and power. Australia and New Zealand also governed some islands. The chief value of these islands was as ports of call and sources of supplies for sailing vessels making the long voyage across the Pacific. Later, they became important landing places for airplanes to refuel. Because of their beauty, warm climate, and the friendliness of their people, Europeans regarded these islands as paradise. Paul Gaugin, a French artist, settled in Tahiti, where he painted brightly colored pictures depicting the joys of island life. French Polynesia, which includes Tahiti, remains a part of France today and sends representatives to the French legislature. New Caledonia, Wallis, and Futuna are also overseas *départements* (the political equivalent of states in the United States) of France.

The western part of New Guinea was part of the Dutch East Indies (today Indonesia). The eastern part of this country is closest to Australia, and the Torres Strait Islands people are related to the Australian Aborigines. British interests began economic ventures on the southern coast of New Guinea and some nearby islands in the late nineteenth century. Then in 1884, a German company moved into the northeastern part of New Guinea. Britain responded by taking the southeastern part, called Papua, which passed to Australia in 1906. In 1921, the League of Nations granted German New Guinea to Australia as a mandate.

Most of the islands were ruled by one power, but there were places where two colonial powers ruled together. On Canton Island, part of the Phoenix Islands, an American Coast Guard officer came ashore and proclaimed, "I claim this land for the United States of America." A British officer, who had been living there for some time, responded, "In the name of His Majesty King George VI, I protest. Come into the shack and have a cup of tea." In such friendly fashion, Britain and the United States ruled Canton until 1979, when it became part of the independent Republic of Kiribati.

The United States also ruled some islands in the region alone—mostly in Micronesia. It had acquired Guam and Hawaii in 1898; Hawaii became a state in 1959. The Caroline Islands, Palau, the Northern Marianas, and the Marshall Islands had all been conquered by Japan during World War II. In 1947, the United Nations turned them over to the United States as a trust territory. Trusteeship meant that they were supposed to be developed and prepared for independence.

Although Australia and New Zealand—the settler colonies—became independent early in the twentieth century, independence came to the smaller islands only after World War II. Their role in World War II was a major factor. The first was Western Samoa, which received independence from New Zealand in 1962. By 1980, eight others had followed: Nauru (1968), Fiji (1970), Tonga (1970), Papua New Guinea (1975), Solomon Islands (1978), Kiribati (1978), Tuvalu (1978), and Vanuatu (1980). All had been British territories, or protectorates or colonies of Australia or New Zealand.

Discussions regarding full self-government for the U.S.-held islands began in 1969. Palau, the Northern Marianas, and the Marshall Islands broke off from the federation of Micronesian states. The Caroline islands of Yap, Truk, Dosrae, and Pohnpei became the independent Federated States of Micronesia in 1983. The Marshall Islands voted to enter free association with the United States. They align their foreign policy with the United States and allow military bases. In return, they receive aid, and their citizens may come to the United States to work. In 1975, the Northern Mariana Islands established a commonwealth in association with the United States. Palau became independent in 1994.

AUSTRALIA AND THE PACIFIC IN THE WORLD

As we have seen, once they knew of its existence, Europeans competed for possessions in the Pacific region. The British began to settle Western Australia because they thought the French had their eyes on it. European powers seized small islands just so no one else could claim them. Later on, the Japanese and the Germans took territories that were not already claimed. Germany lost its colonies after World War I, and Japan lost its after World War II.

The region seemed very far away to Europeans. That, of course, was one reason why the British had originally thought that Australia would make a good penal colony. The French later used New Caledonia for the same purpose.

Australia and New Zealand viewed themselves as outposts of the British Empire. To this day, their flags contain the British Union Jack in the upper left-hand corner. They contributed troops to the British side in both World War I and World War II. In World War I, Australian and New Zealand forces (Anzacs) suffered terrible losses at the Battle of Gallipoli, in Turkey, when they were surrounded by much larger forces of better-armed Turks. The slaughter remains firmly entrenched in the Australian national consciousness.

Europeans referred to East Asia as the "Far East," and people in Australia and New Zealand adopted that worldview. World War II brought the stark realization that the "Far East" was really the "Near North." As Japanese forces pressed south, Darwin in the Northern Territory was bombed. Since then, Australia and New Zealand have developed more interest in their relationships with Asian countries.

After the British evacuation of Dunkirk early in World War II, far-off Australia seemed like a good place to send prisoners-of-war. One of them wrote of his experience:

> I was interned during the well-known internment wave of "Friendly Aliens of Enemy Origin," a temporary measure taken after Dunkirk when they really had the jitters in England. I was interned on 26th June, 1940, and on 10th July of that year I found myself on H.M.T. DUNERA, transporting a bunch of 2500 Internees "somewhere" in the British Empire, most likely a Dominion. We were guarded by a rabble of military criminals—military defaulters, just returned from Dunkirk who had to be punished for one thing or another, and were therefore sent on this guarding expedition while their mates, after return to England, had been given leave. Their Commander . . . closed both eyes and let his men take everything from us we had, including wedding rings, and rip our luggage open with bayonets. We arrived

> in Australia in what we stood in. The matter then gradually became known, and it is to the credit of the British Government—and no other government in the world would have cared about such acts of robbery in wartime—that they court-martialed the ring leaders, and paid £54,000 Sterling damages to us.

Many of these prisoners joined the Australian army and after the war stayed in Australia as permanent residents and citizens.

Italian and Japanese soldiers were imprisoned at a camp near Cowra. To the Japanese, being held captive brought unbearable shame, not only to the soldier but also to the soldier's family. Before dawn on August 4, 1944, 378 of about 1,000 Japanese prisoners broke out of the camp. They thought that if they crossed the hills they could see to the east, a Japanese boat would pick them up on the shore of the Pacific Ocean. They did not realize that the coast was more than 150 miles (more than 250 kilometers) away. Many were killed on the spot; others escaped and committed suicide, and still others were recaptured. After the war, the people of Cowra established a Japanese garden and culture center to build better relations with Japan. Australia's Peace Bell, a replica of the one on the United Nations Plaza in New York, hangs in front of Cowra's town hall in recognition of these efforts.

After the Japanese attack on Pearl Harbor, the United States and its allies fought to retake the islands that Japan had seized. From the Coral Sea, east of Australia, they used the islands of Melanesia as stepping stones to reach the Philippines. The islands of Micronesia led the way toward Japan itself. Some of the most famous battles of World War II were fought in these islands: Guadalcanal in the Solomon Islands, Saipan in the Marianas, and Iwo Jima, for example.

After World War II, the isolation of the Pacific islands became their important strategic characteristic. The United States, Britain, and France needed places to test nuclear

U.S. Marines approach the Japanese-occupied island of Guadalcanal in the Solomon Islands in 1942 during World War II. The Allied Forces used the islands of Micronesia as stepping stones to reach the Japanese in the Philippines.

weapons. The United States used Enewetak and the Bikini Atoll in the Micronesian territory, which it held under UN trusteeship. Britain and the United States conducted joint tests on Christmas Island (now in Kiribati) and at Maralinga in Australia. After Algeria became independent, France shifted its testing site to French Polynesia. Protests against these tests eventually led to the Treaty of Rarotonga, prohibiting such tests, but only the Soviet Union and China signed.

Concerns over nuclear testing also extended to nuclear-powered ships. In 1985, New Zealand declared itself a nuclear-free zone. No nuclear-powered ships would henceforth be allowed to enter New Zealand waters. Consequently, in 1986, the

United States declared that it would no longer offer military protection to New Zealand as provided through the treaty organization ANZUS (Australia New Zealand United States).

In the late twentieth century, American attention was drawn to an emerging region of great economic importance—the Pacific Rim. Faster travel and transportation made the ocean seem smaller, just as the Atlantic Ocean seemed smaller to Europeans after the voyages of discovery beginning in the late fifteenth century. American economic and political interests in East and Southeast Asia grew. Australia, New Zealand, and the United States were members of the Southeast Asia Treaty Organization (SEATO), which was organized in 1954, primarily in defense against Communism. Members disagreed about the role of the United States in Southeast Asia, and the organization disbanded in 1977. Australia contributed troops to the war in Vietnam, and many American service personnel spent rest and recreation leaves in Australia. New Zealand remained more aloof from this venture, opposing the Vietnam War. Similarly, Australia sent forces to the First Gulf War in 1991 and joined the "Coalition of the Willing" to support the United States invasion of Iraq in 2003, whereas New Zealand did not.

Australia and New Zealand were among the 51 original members of the United Nations, and other countries of the region have joined after achieving independence. Australia and New Zealand are also members of APEC (Asia-Pacific Economic Cooperation) and, along with other wealthy countries, of OECD (Organization for Economic Cooperation and Development). Many former British colonies, including Australia and New Zealand, are also members of the (British) Commonwealth of Nations.

GOVERNMENTS

Not surprisingly, the countries of the Pacific region have copied the government systems of their former colonial rulers as they have become independent. They have also added their own features. Some of the new countries are still working on political systems that will democratically represent all the various population groups.

Australia

Australia's government is a mix of the British Parliamentary and the American Congressional system. The framers of the constitution were British, and the constitution was passed as an act of the British Parliament. However, many Australians were familiar with the American system and wanted to incorporate some of its features.

Australia's government, like that of the United States, separates the powers of the legislative, executive, and judicial branches. Its Parliament, or legislature, consists of two houses. The House of Representatives, like its American counterpart, is elected from districts of approximately equal population. Members serve four-year terms. The Senate comprises 12 representatives of each state and two from each territory (Northern Territory and Australia Capital Territory, or Canberra). Like the British House of Lords, it acts as a reviewer rather than an initiator of laws. Senators from the states serve for six years, and one-half the body is elected every three years. Senators from the territories serve three-year terms.

State governments are structured much like the federal government. All, except for Queensland which has one, have two legislative chambers that are responsible for health, housing, education, justice, and transportation. The federal government has the most power to raise money from taxes, however, so states must rely on federal grants to carry out their functions. Local government (Australia has no counties) performs such functions as trash collection, street maintenance, and establishing and enforcing building codes.

Voting is mandatory in Australia. Because of the complex ways in which officeholders are chosen, voters must rank all the candidates on the ballot in order of preference. Mapping voting districts is very complicated because of the enormous differences in population density. The same number of people may live in one city block in Sydney as in a huge expanse of the outback. Each vote in the outback can therefore have more power. Since the outback tends to be more conservative than the cities, the result is the election of more conservative officials.

Australia recognizes Queen Elizabeth of the United Kingdom as its head of state, despite various attempts to make the country into a republic. Her representative in Australia is the governor general, who approves the laws that Parliament passes. The party that has the most members of the House of Representatives selects the prime minister, who in turn selects members of the cabinet.

At the time of Confederation, Australia chose a site for a new, planned capital called Canberra (Aboriginal for "meeting place") between the two major cities of Sydney and Melbourne. Work began on its construction in 1911 after an American, Walter Burley Griffin, won the design competition. The city occupies two sides of artificial Lake Burley Griffin, one side for government buildings and one for the commercial and residential city. Each side is laid out in a series of concentric circles with major roads forming the spokes of a wheel. Parliament House, opened in 1988, forms the apex of the Parliamentary Triangle. It is partly underground and was built to be accessible to the public. To the west of Parliament House is the embassy district. Each country has designed its embassy to reflect its own culture and architecture. The United States embassy uses themes from the colonial buildings of Williamsburg, Virginia.

New Zealand

New Zealand, too, has a government that is patterned after the British Parliamentary system. Like Britain, it has no constitution. The Treaty of Waitangi and various court rulings form the basis of government. The Constitution Act of 1986 brought together the most important points of these documents.

New Zealand's Parliament has only one legislative chamber, the House of Representatives. Members serve three-year terms. There are 120 members, 69 elected from single-member districts (including those reserved for Maori representatives) and 51 proportional seats chosen according to the parties of the elected members. This system gives greater voice to minor political parties. In addition to all New Zealanders 18 and older, foreigners who have permanent residence and have lived in New Zealand for a year also may vote.

The leader of the party with the most members in Parliament becomes the prime minister and appoints the cabinet. All cabinet members must be members of Parliament. The cabinet plus the governor general (appointed by Queen Elizabeth II of England, who is the head of state) comprise the government, which sets the country's policies. The governor general approves laws passed by Parliament.

New Zealand does not have states. For administrative purposes, it is divided into 16 regions. These regions are further divided into districts.

Wellington, at the southern end of North Island, became New Zealand's capital in 1865. People in South Island had been complaining about the difficulty of traveling the distance to Auckland, so the capital was moved to the more central location. Parliament House was built in 1922, and the House of Representatives' meeting chamber was modeled after the House of Commons in London. Next door, a modern building, called the "Beehive" and designed by the British architect Sir Basil Spence, was built between 1964 and 1981. It houses government offices and the meeting room of the Cabinet.

Pacific Islands

As we have seen, the smaller islands of the Pacific region have become independent much more recently. A few are still ruled by the United States, France, Australia, or New Zealand. As these countries have established independent governments, they have copied some elements from their former rulers. They have also added features from their traditional cultures. Fiji and Samoa are examples.

In Fiji, the traditional Great Council of Chiefs continues to be part of the government. The Fiji Constitution Amendment Act 1997 provides for a House of Representatives with 71 members. Of these, 46 members represent districts called ridings, with 23 for Fijians, 19 for Indo-Fijians, 3 for general electors (Europeans, Chinese, etc.), and 1 for Rotumans. The party with the largest number of members names the prime minister, and any party with eight members has a right to a place in the Cabinet. Voting is compulsory. The Senate has 32 members, with 14 appointed by the Great Council of Chiefs, 9 by the prime minister, 8 by the leader of the opposition party, and 1 by the Council of Rotuma. The Great Council of Chiefs also names Fiji's president, who serves for five years.

Nevertheless, there remain conflicts, from both ethnic and economic sources, between the various groups. The first coup in the region was in Fiji in 1987. Although the general who seized power was Fijian and the leaders of the government he overturned were Indo-Fijians (Fijians whose ancestors came from India), the issues were really about land and power. Traditional Fijian chiefs continue to hold powerful positions, and Indo-Fijians protest restrictions on their owning land. Disagreement between Fijians who wanted more ties and identification with Melanesia and those who saw the country as Polynesian contributed to the conflict. A second coup in 1987 made Fiji a republic.

New elections were held in 1992, and in 1997 a new constitution was passed. It provided for fewer seats in Parliament to be reserved for Fijians, and voting across racial lines was instituted for another third of the seats. The cabinet would be required to represent all the political parties. Nearly half the members of the Senate would be appointed by the Great Council of Chiefs, the traditional Fijian leaders. This constitution took effect in 1998.

Fijian and Indian residents line up to vote in the general elections on the last day of polling in Suva, Fiji, September 1, 2001. Voting in Fiji's general election took several days because there are more than 300 islands scattered throughout the republic.

The new government lasted until 2000, when another coup took place. In addition to previous arguments was a disagreement about who should market Fiji's valuable mahogany production overseas. The arguments and illegal efforts to revise the 1997 constitution continue. The series of coups and conflicts has damaged the country's economy and increased the gap between rich and poor.

Another new country that has faced conflicts is Samoa. In 2003, Australia, in consultation with other South Pacific Forum countries, sent peacekeeping forces to Samoa. Western Samoa had been a German colony, but after World War I, New Zealand took it over as a mandate of the League of Nations and then as a trusteeship of the United Nations. The country became independent in 1962 and dropped "Western" from its name in 1997. Samoa has only one chamber in its legislature, the Legislative Assembly (Fono). Members serve for five years. Of the 49 members, 47 are elected by village-based districts and 2 by people who are not part of villages. Only chiefs may represent village districts. The Fono elects the chief of state. The leader of the party with the most seats in the Fono becomes prime minister by appointment by the chief of state and approval of the Fono.

As distances seem to shrink with modern communications and transportation, the Pacific countries become more tied to the world, and more important to other nations both economically and politically. We hear little about these countries in the news because Australia and New Zealand are peaceful and prosperous, and Americans regard the Pacific islands as having little influence in world affairs. They do, however, play a role, sometimes if only to remind other nations of different viewpoints on world issues.

CHAPTER 6

Economy

Australia's Aborigines found what they needed for living in their immediate environment, although they traded among themselves for other goods. The peoples of the islands raised crops and animals, and established wide-ranging trade networks to obtain what they needed.

Once Europeans settled this region, they desired products from the new factories in their home countries. They also needed something they could sell in Europe to earn a living. Once these countries were settled, their economies depended on their ability to supply what people in other parts of the world wanted. "Globalization" here is more than 200 years old.

AUSTRALIA AND NEW ZEALAND

Europeans first came to Australia as prisoners and their guards. These settlers brought some supplies with them, but these were quickly used up. They found nothing in Australia acceptable as food, although they later learned to eat kangaroo meat, which tastes much like beef.

Agriculture

At first, the British settlers tried to produce goods that were needed on ships of the Royal Navy and on those of whalers and seal hunters. Eastern Australia did not have tall trees that could be used for ships' masts, however, nor did it have anything that could be woven into linen for sails. Even the Norfolk pine and wild flax on Norfolk Island proved unsuitable. The settlers hardly had enough food for themselves—and certainly no surplus to sell to sailors. What could they produce in their new dry, flat country that seemed to have infertile soils?

Some animals and grain seeds had been brought from Britain to provide for their own needs. They soon discovered that grain would grow well, especially west of the Great Dividing Range. This land was also good for pasturing animals. The British settlers improved the pastureland by adding European grasses. In 1810, they introduced Merino sheep, which have very long, soft wool. As settlement spread north along the east coast of Australia, sugar plantations were established in subtropical coastal Queensland.

Cattle and sheep are butchered and eaten as beef and lamb (or mutton). Cows also provide leather, and sheep provide wool. Because meat would spoil on the long voyage to Europe, Australia's early exports were grains, hides, and wool. Europe needed these products, because the people who worked in its new, growing factories did not produce their own food. They had to buy it. Furthermore, the population was growing, so there were more people to be fed and less land to use for farming. Australian (as well as North American) wheat helped to meet these needs for food.

Those same factories were hungry for raw materials, including wool. Just as there was not enough land in Great Britain to raise the wheat to feed English factory workers, there was not enough land there on which to pasture sheep to meet the increased needs of the textile mills and factories manufacturing woolen goods. Both Australia and New Zealand became major wool-producing lands. New Zealand today has about 4 million people—and 70 million sheep!

In the late nineteenth century came the invention of refrigerated ships, making it possible to send meat from these distant lands to Europe. But somebody else had beaten the Australians and New Zealanders to it—the Argentinians in South America, aided by British investment in railroads and ports. However, after World War II, North Americans began eating more meat than ever, and Australia and New Zealand had found a new market. New Zealand is a major supplier of lamb to Canada, for example.

Wheat, cattle, and sheep are produced mainly in Australia's outback, especially in the Great Artesian Basin. The wetter parts, in the east, are used primarily to graze sheep. The drier parts are cattle ranches, called "stations" in Australia, where cattle are born and spend the first part of their lives. Cattle have longer legs and can walk farther to find water than can sheep. Nevertheless, it takes a lot of this land of sparse vegetation to support cattle. The stations are huge—as much as one million acres (440,000 hectares). When the cattle are full-sized, they are sent to wetter regions, where grain can be grown, to be fattened for market.

With the stations so huge, people live far apart. On the six-hour drive from Alice Springs to Yulara (the accommodations for Uluru-Kata Tjuta National Park), there is not a single town, just a few "road houses," with a gas station and a small shop selling snacks and a few other items.

Australians have had to be very innovative to ensure that people living in the outback receive such services as education

John Davidson, left, and Dave Saunders work cattle at Bullo River Station in the Australian outback. Stations such as this one can be as large as one million acres.

and health care. Two institutions, both with headquarters in Alice Springs, help meet these needs. The first is the School of the Air. It is a little like homeschooling, but the students spend a part of each day talking with their teacher and "classmates" via two-way radio. Their work is on display at the School of the Air headquarters in Alice Springs. The Royal Flying Doctor Service brings medical care to stations in the outback. If necessary, the planes can also transport patients to Alice Springs for hospital care. Today, of course, people in the outback receive transmissions of radio and television programs as well as the Internet, so they are much less isolated than they were when settlement began, or even several decades ago.

New Zealand in the first days of European settlement was a supply point for whalers and seal hunters. It had tall trees for masts, and it also had fruits and vegetables. The Maori were farmers, many of whom would sell food to Europeans in return for manufactured goods like nails and red paint. Today, in addition to sheep, New Zealand produces cattle (mostly dairy cattle). With a cooler, wetter climate than Australia's, the country has ideal conditions for dairy farming. Because fresh milk would spoil on the long voyages to markets in Europe or North America, New Zealand milk is made into butter and cheese, as well as dry milk powder, for shipping. In the late twentieth century, especially with new trading relations with China, New Zealand's Dairy Marketing Board found new markets for dairy products in Asia. East Asians do not drink milk, and cheese is not one of their traditional foods. But dairy products are becoming more popular, especially yogurt and ice cream—and cheese-topped pizza. Asian children are drinking more milk, to the great benefit of their teeth and bones. The growing tourism business in East Asia is another market for New Zealand dairy products.

New Zealand also began to meet another demand from Asia: Deer antlers are an important ingredient in traditional Chinese medicine. New Zealand farmers now pasture deer, not just for their meat (venison), but also for their antlers.

New Zealand's cool, wet climate also makes it an ideal place to grow middle-latitude fruits such as apples, pears, and kiwifruit. Because in New Zealand it is summer when in the Northern Hemisphere it is winter, the country can send these fruits to places that are not producing them at that time. Since the kiwi bird is the national symbol of New Zealand, what better place to produce kiwifruit, even though it is actually native to China.

Mining

Australia's early European settlers did not know that they had stumbled upon one of the places on earth richest in minerals. The land was flat and dry, but it was the core of an ancient tec-

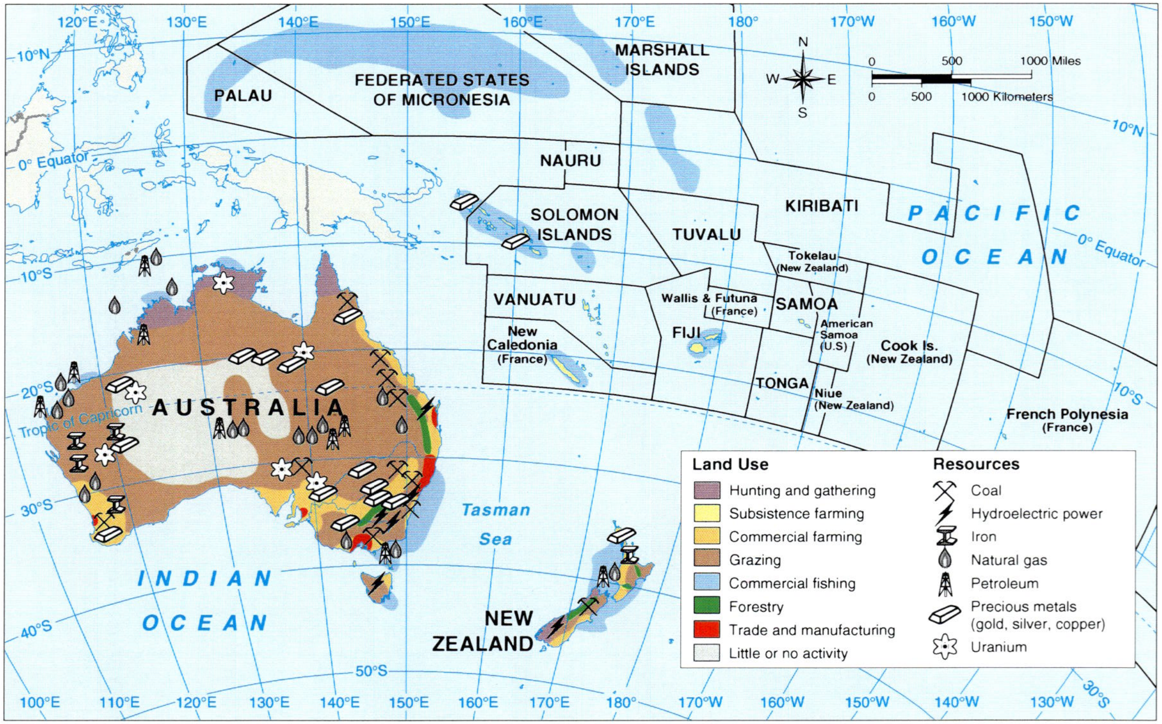

Australia and New Zealand are significant producers of cattle, sheep, and wheat. They are also rich in natural resources. The Pacific islands were originally developed by the Europeans to be producers of tropical crops such as pineapple, papaya, and other tropical fruits, as well as sugar cane and coconuts. Following independence, trade patterns did not change significantly.

tonic plate and rich in gold, silver, iron, manganese, lead, zinc, and many other essential resources. Farther east, where layers of younger rock lay on top of the ancient granites, important fossil fuels—coal, petroleum, and natural gas—could be found.

Australia's first gold strike occurred in Victoria in 1851. It caused a gold rush similar to the one in California two years earlier, except that there were fewer people within range to get there. The discovery attracted enough free settlers, however, that the transportation of criminals as a way to occupy the land ended. Today, important gold-mining centers include Broken Hill in western New South Wales, Port Hedland and Kalgoorlie in Western Australia, and Mt. Isa in western Queensland.

Exploitation of Australia's other mineral wealth, less glamorous but more important economically, had to wait until the late twentieth century. Iron ore and aluminum (made from deposits of bauxite) have found a big market in the reviving industries of post–World War II Japan. There are also deposits of copper, uranium, and other industrial minerals. Gems include diamonds and the opals for which Australia is famous. Almost all of these deposits are found in the dry outback, far from other centers of population. The mining towns exist only because there is mineral wealth to exploit.

Manufacturing

In the early twentieth century, war interfered with shipments of manufactured goods from Europe. In the 1930s, a worldwide economic depression destroyed the markets for Australian and New Zealand products. They had factories to process agricultural and mineral products for export, but then they had to buy more expensive finished items from abroad. Citizens of both countries began to ask, "Why not make our own?"

The primary problem hindering the development of manufacturing industries in both countries was that they had small populations. Even though the standard of living was high and people had disposable income (spending money), there just were not enough of them. Investors were reluctant to build a factory to supply goods for so few people. Both countries encouraged the development of industry by setting very high tariffs (taxes) on imported goods. If a company wanted to earn money from selling manufactured products to Australians and New Zealanders, it was going to have to make them there. Automobile companies began to build assembly plants, primarily in cities, where people lived who would buy cars. The companies shipped all the parts of the cars, like kits, to Australia and New Zealand, and then the factories there just put them together. They were considered to be made within the country, and the assembly-line workers had jobs.

Campbell Soup Company, wanting to expand its market to these countries, bought a food-processing factory in Australia. The factory, at Shepparton, Victoria, was surrounded by a region of fruit and vegetable farming. From there, it could supply the region with canned soup and other products.

This system worked for a while, but in the late twentieth century, Australia's and New Zealand's traditional market—Great Britain—became more connected with the continent of Europe. The special trade ties to Australia and New Zealand began to fray. The countries needed new markets, but countries like the United States, as well as the newly formed European Union, demanded that these markets be open to their products, too. No longer was it possible to protect the small factories that were making goods just for Australia and New Zealand from imports. The imports were less expensive because wages were so much lower in countries such as China, Malaysia, and India.

Clothing was one of the first industries to feel the effects. Clothing is one of the first items that a newly industrializing country makes. The raw materials are cheap and easily available, the machinery is fairly simple and requires little training to use, and everyone needs the product. Furthermore, much of the labor force is women, who already know how to sew because they have long made clothes for their families. The workers in

A clothing worker sews wet suits. Imports, especially in the clothing industry, are less expensive because wages are much lower in countries such as China, Malaysia, and India. Many New Zealanders lost their jobs to replacements who can work for lower wages.

New Zealand's clothing plants lost their jobs. Some of their replacements were people from the Pacific islands who had come to New Zealand looking for jobs. Some were Pacific islanders who stayed in their homelands and worked in foreign-owned factories there.

New Zealand consumers were happy with the arrangement, which brought them much more variety in clothing at much lower prices. And not all the clothing companies suffered. Some turned to making high-quality items, especially rainwear and clothes for sports and for camping. Products made from sheepskin were another specialty.

The automobile industry became more consolidated in cities, and some factories closed. Most of the factories are still owned by foreign companies, but more of the manufacturing process is carried out in Australia and New Zealand. Some of the vehicles are now exported. On the other hand, used cars are being imported—from Japan where, as in Australia and New Zealand, they also drive on the left side of the road.

Services

Most people in Australia and New Zealand work in the service industry. Instead of making a physical product, they do something for someone: teach students, help people get or stay well, drive trucks and buses, or create advertising for companies. Both countries have excellent schools, and both have good health care, to which everyone is entitled by law. Both countries have excellent transportation systems, although some of the roads in Australia's outback are not paved (or "sealed," as they say). The railroad north from Adelaide that ended at Alice Springs was extended to Darwin. The parallel Stuart Highway features "truck trains," with each truck pulling two or three huge trailers.

With the advent of long-distance travel by jet aircraft in the latter part of the twentieth century, Australia and New Zealand began to feel less culturally isolated. European orchestras, artists, dance and opera companies, singers, world-class athletes, and other performers could tour the countries. And these visitors inspired young artists in those countries to come to Europe or America. Melbourne hosted the Olympics in 1956 and Sydney in 2000.

After Melbourne hosted the Olympics, Sydney felt it had to have something dramatic of its own. It decided to build an opera house. Jørn Utzon won the design competition, and the venue was under construction from 1959 to 1973. The completed building contains both an opera house and a concert hall, as well as smaller rooms and a long monumental flight of steps that can be used for outdoor performances. It has become a symbol for Sydney and for all of Australia, showing how the country has come to the cultural forefront.

Both Australia and New Zealand, with their dramatic scenery, have attracted movie makers. In 1993, the New Zealand story *The Piano* was filmed in Australia. In 2001, moviegoers saw New Zealand's beauty in the first segment of the *Lord of the Rings* trilogy. Masterpiece Theatre features have included *A Town Like Alice* by Nevil Shute and *The Road from Coorain* by Jill Ker Conway, both about Australia.

Despite air travel, both Australia and New Zealand suffer as tourist destinations because of their great distance from major sources of travelers. Increasing numbers of Japanese come to visit, mostly on organized tours, as do Europeans and Americans. Nevertheless, Australia receives between three and four million tourists each year, and New Zealand just over one million (about the same as Hawaii). In Australia, the Great Barrier Reef, Sydney, and Uluru (Ayers Rock) are the most popular destinations. In New Zealand, although hiking and camping are popular, Auckland and Rotorua with its geysers and hot springs are the biggest attractions. South Island features ski resorts. Because of seasonal differences, these are very popular to skiers escaping the Northern Hemisphere's summer season.

The Pacific Islands

The tropical islands of the Pacific do not have the wide-open spaces or the climate to raise wheat, cattle, and sheep. In the past, they supplied a different kind of product to the growing industrial populations of the homelands of their European rulers. Europe is too cold to grow tropical crops such as pineapple, papaya, and other tropical fruits, as well as sugarcane and coconuts. That continent does not have tropical trees like mahogany or sandalwood. Yet, rising incomes in Europe allowed people, especially the newly rich owners of industry, to buy these items. Consequently, Europeans went to the Pacific islands to establish plantations and lumbering operations. The sugar plantations in Queensland, Australia, were founded for similar reasons.

On many of the islands, local people provided a labor force. In other cases, the Europeans imported workers from other places. People from South Asia were brought to Fiji, and Melanesians were taken to Queensland, Australia, to work in the sugarcane fields. The plantations shipped their products back to Europe, and the profits went to the European owners. The owners lived in big houses, had servants, and sent their children to school in Europe. They imported European goods. Very few factories, beyond plants to process goods for shipment, were built in these island colonies. Following independence, the trade patterns changed very little. The islands still produce coconuts, copra (dried coconut meat), coconut oil, and tropical fruits for export. They import manufactured goods such as vehicles, machinery, and computers.

The Pacific islands were formed by volcanic action, and only a few have any mineral wealth. Nauru is virtually one big pile of phosphate, which is important in making fertilizer. In fact, the small island country is being "eaten away" by the mining of this resource! New Caledonia has huge nickel deposits. On both islands, destructive mining practices have left the islands decimated. Papua New Guinea, where rocks were formed by the crumpling of the edge of the Indo-Australia tectonic plate, deposits of gold and copper were found. It may well harbor other minerals, as well, but not much of it has been thoroughly explored by geologists.

The people of the Pacific islands have fished in the surrounding waters for as long as they have lived there. Fishing is still an important part of their livelihood and food supply, and they also export fish. American Samoa, for example, exports canned tuna fish. French Polynesia exports another resource from the sea: pearls.

Some islands, such as Tonga, Tuvalu, and Pitcairn, earn money performing a government function. Like other independent countries, they operate a postal service and produce stamps. These countries, however, advertise their stamps to people overseas, who will buy them for collections, not to send mail. If microstates of Europe, like Vatican City and Liechtenstein, can sell their beautiful stamps, why not make elaborate stamps to sell to collectors around the world? Although many stamp collectors regard these stamps as less than authentic because their main purpose is not to pay postage, the countries do earn some money from the venture.

Offering beautiful scenery, sandy beaches, an exotic culture, and balmy tropical weather, the Pacific islands have tried to attract more tourists. Each year, between 100,000 and 500,000 tourists come to French Polynesia, primarily to the beautiful tropical island of Tahiti. More come to Fiji, which has better connections to North America. New Caledonia, which is closer to Australia, also attracts more tourists. Guam, an American island that is relatively close to Japan, receives over a half-million tourists a year. The other island countries have far fewer visitors.

Tourists bring income to the islands, but many of the facilities that serve them are owned by foreign companies. The managers may also be foreigners. The jobs available to local people are housekeeping and serving food, which are low-paying. Many of the resorts are self-contained; that is, they provide everything tourist visitors need. As a result, the tourists' experience of the island is just of an enclave of the wealthy country from which they came. Very rarely is there even transportation to other places, except the airport. Apart from some performances of traditional singing and dancing, and perhaps a lecture on the history and culture of the island, the tourists might as well have visited a beach resort in their own countries. Cultural traditions of the island are reduced to a show for tourists, who are unfamiliar with their meanings,

Dancers perform for visitors at the Micronesian Culture Center, State of Pompei, South Pacific. While the Pacific islands attract many visitors, most tourist facilities are controlled by foreign companies. As a result, the people of the islands experience little economic benefit.

and profits from the whole enterprise go back to the country of the corporation's owner.

The Pacific islands did not experience the building of factories in the early twentieth century. Their colonial rulers, who wanted to sell goods from the home countries, did not allow them to develop. Now that the countries are independent, many of them are trying to attract factories in order to provide better-paying jobs for their citizens. Setting up a factory requires investors, and that funding has come from wealthy countries, including Australia, New Zealand, and the United States. New Zealand investors, for example, have set up clothing factories in Fiji, where wages are lower than they are in New Zealand. American companies produce manufactured goods, including clothing, in the Northern Marianas. Like tourist facilities, these factories send their profits back to the countries of their owners. Similarly, many of the banks in the Pacific islands are branches of banks in wealthy countries. Banks in Fiji, for example, are branches of banks in Australia and New Zealand.

Like the characteristics of populations, the economic systems of Australia and the Pacific are different in the countries where Europeans settled in large numbers than they are in those to which only a few entrepreneurs came. All these countries export products to markets in the Northern Hemisphere, but the products vary—so do the kinds of jobs people hold and the lives they live. "Globalization" affects them all, but in different ways.

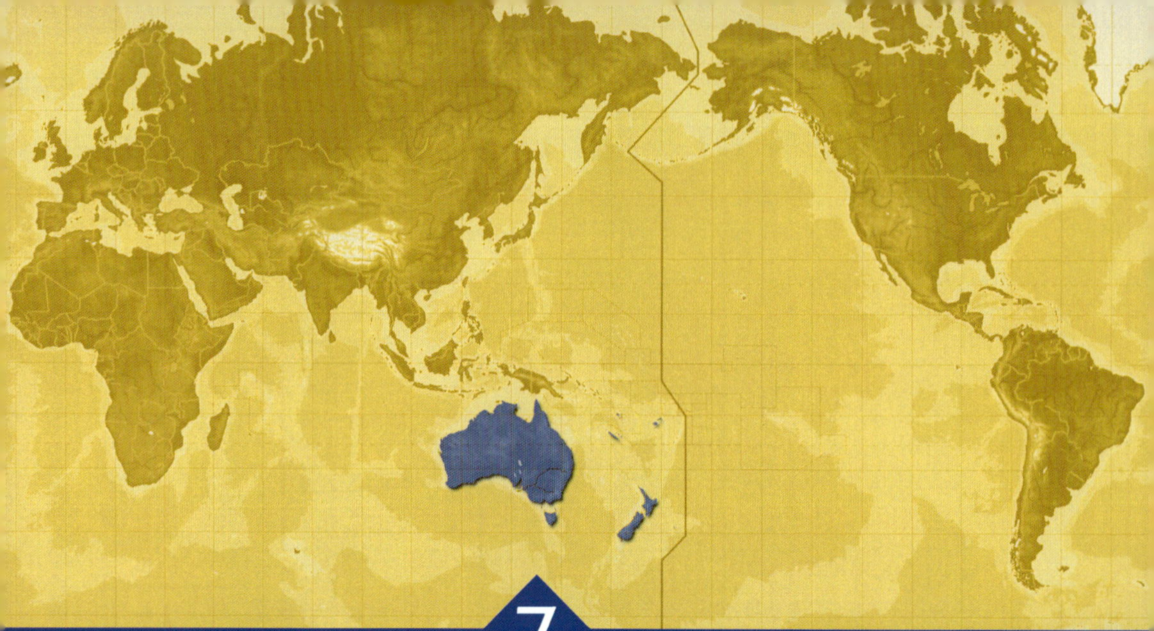

CHAPTER 7

Regional Contrasts

Australia and the Pacific islands have important features in common. They all feel the effects of the Pacific, the world's largest ocean. The region is far away from Europe, but its life is in many ways impacted by Europe.

In other ways, the parts of this region are different. Australia and New Zealand are wealthy countries where most people enjoy a high standard of living and stable, democratic political systems. The Pacific island countries have lower levels of well-being, and they are still developing political systems that will serve their needs and function democratically.

AUSTRALIA AND NEW ZEALAND

Australia and New Zealand are located in the middle latitudes. When settling the area, Europeans regarded these countries as acceptable places to live. There they encountered no strange tropical diseases, and there seemed to be few native people with whom they had to contend. In both Australia and New Zealand, the most powerful part of the population was the descendents of European settlers. The settlers produced goods to send to Europe that earned them a decent living. By the early twentieth century, in fact, Australians and "Kiwis" were living better than Europeans. Based on models they knew, they developed efficient, democratic forms of government that gave them authority over their own affairs while retaining loyalty to the British monarch. Nevertheless, in both countries, the conditions of the native peoples continue to present a challenge.

Australia

Australia is the only country in the world that is also a continent. Most of it is the core of the Indo-Australia Tectonic Plate. Australia is the world's flattest continent. The only mountains follow the east coast, where the plate collided with the Pacific Plate and crumpled. Even these mountains are not very high. Just to their west, the old granite core of the Indo-Australian Plate is overlain by layers of more recently formed rocks.

Australia's latitude means that most of it gets very little rain at any time of year. Furthermore, the mountains along the east coast form a barrier to winds blowing off the Pacific Ocean. As these winds are pushed upward over the mountains, they lose their moisture as precipitation on the coast side of the mountains. The result is that most of Australia is dry—it is the world's driest inhabited continent. Other than in the sparsely settled tropical far north, only the land immediately west of the mountains in the Great Artesian Basin has reliable water throughout the year. A small area of Western Australia, around Perth, has rainfall in the winter. The continent is large enough that its interior experiences sizable differences between summer and winter temperatures. Summer in the interior, often called the "Red Center," is extremely hot and dry; winter is mild and can be quite chilly.

The first people in Australia, the Aborigines, found the land so rich that they could simply hunt and gather what they needed. When resources in one place ran out, they moved to a new location. There was never any need to plant crops or herd animals so that what they wanted would be available. Life's necessities, for them, were available in the places they occupied, and without much effort. The land was expansive, and there was plenty of room for everyone to find food and other necessities. They also had little need for political hierarchy or government.

As you have seen, the first European settlers were literally a bunch of criminals and their guards—not exactly the sort of group that one would predict would build a strong, prosperous, democratic country. In the early days, they struggled. They expected supplies of food and other necessities to come from England, and few of them had the kinds of skills needed to build a colony. They had no idea how to use the plants and animals they found. Soils in the place where they first landed were unsuitable for growing European crops. Starvation was a constant companion for the first few years.

Nevertheless, the British government seems to have wanted the colony to succeed. Officers and prisoners on the fleets received daily doses of citrus fruit, so that they would not contract scurvy. The ruling country did send supply ships, even if some of them never reached Australia. It also sent competent rulers for the colony.

Eventually, farms were established; these were generally owned by the guards and worked by the convicts until they had served out their sentences. Former convicts could also receive land grants. The colony began to discover crops and animals that would thrive in the new environment and sell well in Europe. Valuable mineral resources were found.

The hard early years of European settlement in Australia left their mark. Australians believe strongly in individual hard work and the strength to deal with a difficult and unpredictable environment. Yet, their history of hardships has also given them a sense of working together and helping each other—of "mateship." This need to care for each other extends to government and public services. Publicly financed education, health care, transportation, and social welfare are important in Australia.

Since the late twentieth century, Australians have been more welcoming of Asian immigrants. The country has thus become multicultural and greatly enriched. With faster transportation and communication, many cultural influences flood in, from American and British television programs and movies to singers, symphonies, and opera companies. Australia has twice hosted the Olympics.

Land use regions of Australia look like the rings of an onion. The outer ring, along the north, east, and south coast (including Tasmania), and around Perth in the west, gets the most rain. In the north are tropical rain forests and savannas, areas of very sparse population and limited access by surface linkages. The rest of this coastal area, except for breaks in the northwest and in the south, has some forests. It also has Australia's fruit and vegetable farms and dairying. Queensland's tropical coastal plain has plantations producing sugarcane. Inside this ring, too, is Australia's wheat-farming and grazing land. Sheep and wheat are raised closer to the Great Dividing Range, where the Great Artesian Basin provides a reliable water supply. Here cattle are fattened for market. Cattle-breeding takes place in the next ring inward, which is drier. In the center, land is too dry for any kind of farming. Much of the land is Aboriginal reserves, as are large parts of the tropical north.

Most Australians, like people in other wealthy countries, live in cities and practice nonagricultural occupations. Except for the capital of Canberra, Australia's cities are located along the coast, especially along the "Boomerang" Coast of the east and southeast. The largest inland town is Alice Springs, Northern Territory, which began as a telegraph relay station and is today a service center for the outback and the entry point for visitors to Uluṟu (Ayers Rock). Perth, Western Australia, takes advantage of nontropical, seasonal rainfall. It holds the distinction of being the most isolated large city (with about 1.2 million people) on Earth.

The Aborigines have not shared to the same degree in the country's general prosperity. Because the Aborigines traditionally moved around in search of food and other needs, the Europeans did not regard them as landowners—or even sometimes as humans. Furthermore, European diseases to which the Aborigines had no immunity killed thousands. As European settlement spread, the Aborigines were pushed out of the lands that Europeans wanted for farming. The spears of the resisting Aborigines were no match for European firearms, and many died in wars. Without their traditional lands, Aborigines' age-old way of life crumbled, leaving them mentally and socially "adrift" between two cultures.

A few Aborigines, such as the tennis star Yvonne Goolagong, have adopted European culture and found success. Others work on cattle and sheep stations or in Australia's cities. Most, however, live on reservations in Northern Territory and Western Australia. A very few can live as their ancestors did, hunting and gathering in the outback, and a few others work at such establishments as Uluṟu-Kata Tjuta National Park, or they create traditional arts and crafts and sell them to tourists and white Australians. For most, rates of poverty, illiteracy, alcoholism, suicide, and infant mortality continue to be considerably higher than those of non-Aboriginal Australians. The country continues to face this challenge.

New Zealand

New Zealand resembles the other Pacific islands in that it is volcanic in origin. However, it is much larger than the other island countries, and it is located in the middle latitudes. Its volcanic origins show in the hilly landscape, hot springs and geysers, and volcanic eruptions and earthquakes that continue to take place.

Because the country is farther south than Australia, New Zealand has a cooler and wetter climate. The islands are small enough that winds from any direction come from water and bring precipitation—snow in winter on South Island. Temperatures are cool in summer and mild in winter, especially on North Island. The Polynesian settlers found they had to make some adjustments in the crops they grew. The British, however, felt right at home in a climate that was similar to what they had left behind.

A few of the first European settlers in New Zealand were former convicts from Australia, but most were traders supplying whaling and seal-hunting ships. In any case, New Zealand was never a penal colony. The people that the Europeans encountered there were also quite different. They were Polynesians who had developed a sophisticated farming society with wide trading networks and a social and political hierarchy. The Maori traded with the Europeans, supplying food and other items in return for goods that they highly desired, especially iron nails and tools, and red paint and cloth. The Maori and the British signed the Treaty of Waitangi in 1840, giving the British sovereignty over the colony but allowing the Maori to keep their land.

Although this treaty has been broken over the years as larger numbers of Europeans moved in and took land, the Maori have always been more equal partners in the country than the Aborigines have been in Australia. Many intermarried with Pakeha, as they call non-Maori New Zealanders, and became assimilated into the mainstream society. They do not live on reservations. Their situation is not perfectly equal to that of Pakeha, however, as on average they have lower incomes and education levels. The country still has work to do, and Maori land claims are particularly complicated and tricky to settle.

New Zealanders of all backgrounds, like Australians, have developed a prosperous country by supplying food and raw ma-

This is a view through the Maori meeting hall and gate, University of Auckland. The Maori were Polynesians who had developed a sophisticated farming society with wide trading networks and a social and political hierarchy. They have always been more equal partners in the country than the Aborigines have been in Australia.

terials to industrialized countries. Changing global trade relations have meant finding new markets and selling these products in different forms—for example, selling protein and powdered milk in place of some of the butter and cheese that have been the traditional exports.

Politically, too, New Zealand has built a strong democracy, while remaining loyal to the British monarchy. While Australia periodically debates becoming a republic with a president instead of the Queen of England as head, New Zealand is quite satisfied to leave things as they are. All newcomers becoming citizens of New Zealand swear allegiance to the Queen.

Nevertheless, New Zealand makes its own decisions about its relations with other countries. It was the first country in the world to grant the vote to women, and it has declared itself a nuclear-free zone. Not even nuclear-powered ships are permitted in its waters. Whereas Australia joined the coalition of countries supporting the invasion of Iraq in 2003, New Zealand did not.

PACIFIC ISLANDS

The Pacific islands, including Papua New Guinea as well as the small islands, represent the less developed world. Their few European settlers became owners of plantations. The role of plantations was to ship tropical products back to Europe, using local labor and land. The owners always considered themselves Europeans more than they were citizens of the islands. The islands remained colonies or trust territories much longer than Australia and New Zealand, and some are still dependent on European countries or the United States.

Based on the size of the islands and the ethnicity of the people, we can divide the Pacific islands into three major groups. You will recall that the group closest to Southeast Asia is Melanesia. The name means "black islands" and comes from the dark skin coloring of the people. East of Melanesia is Polynesia ("many islands"). The "tall" islands in this group are the tops of volcanoes and have ample rainfall and forests. The "low" islands are coral atolls and suffer from drought. North of these two groups, closest to East Asia, is Micronesia ("small islands"). Most of these islands, besides being small, are low (with Guam as an exception). All three groups of islands face the same economic and cultural situation.

As the islands came under European rule, they supplied the rulers' homelands with tropical products such as coconuts (and copra and coconut oil) and tropical fruits and woods. Nauru and New Caledonia proved to have minerals that Europeans found valuable. The islands were also useful as supply stations for ships and later for airplanes crossing the Pacific. The European rulers prohibited the building of factories because they wanted the islands to purchase manufactured goods from Europe's own industries.

The Pacific islands produce coconuts and tropical fruits and woods. The European rulers prohibited the building of factories because they wanted the islanders to purchase manufactured goods from Europe's own industries.

Today, many of the exports from the Pacific islands continue to be products of plantations and in a few cases from mines, forests, and the sea. Some have been moderately successful in exploiting their resources of scenery, beaches, and warm weather and attracting tourists. However, they are distant from large numbers of potential tourists, and many of them lack good transportation connections. With the advent of long-distance jet aircraft, they are no longer valuable as landing places; the planes can fly all the way across the Pacific without needing to stop. In areas where tourists do visit, the traditional culture becomes another commodity to buy in the form of tickets to staged performances.

At the dawn of the twenty-first century, all these areas face challenges related to their location, their cultures and ethnic groups, their resources, and their economic and political life. More and more of these issues relate to the rest of the world, to "globalization."

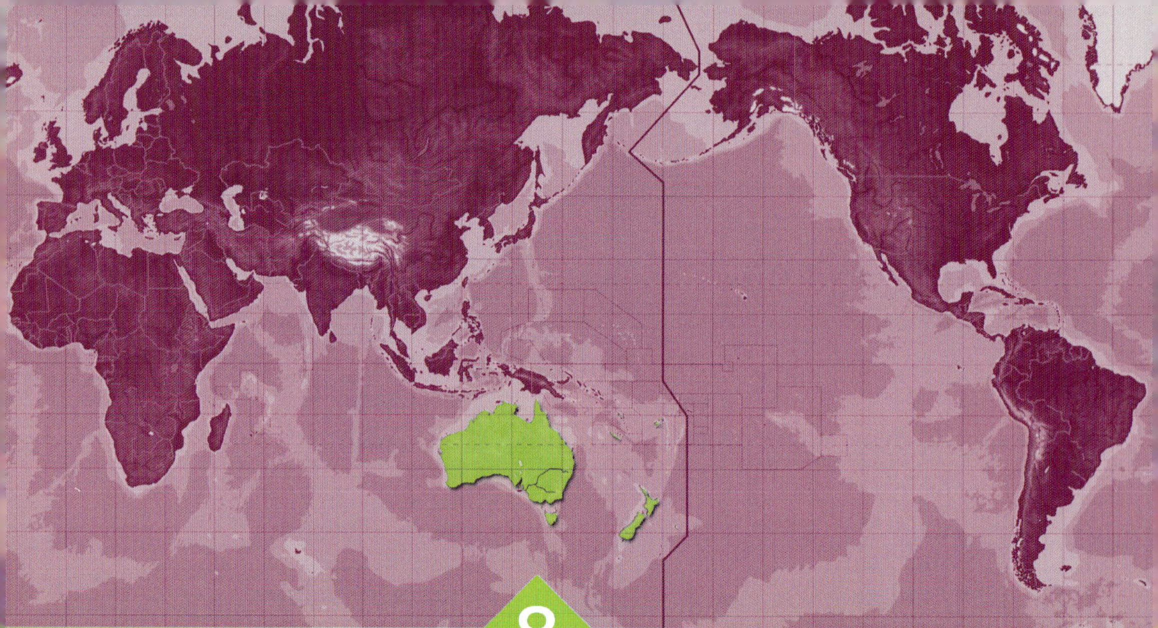

CHAPTER 8

Australia and the Pacific Islands Look Ahead

The Pacific Ocean and distance from the powerful countries of the United States and Europe have shaped the past and present of Australia and the Pacific, and these same forces will continue to shape the future. All the countries face environmental, cultural, economic, and political challenges as the twenty-first century begins.

ENVIRONMENT

Australia was the first place in the world where the effects of damage to the atmosphere's ozone layer were first apparent. Australians love the outdoors; they are real sun worshippers. Christmas comes in mid-summer, and the Australian way of celebrating is to go to the beach. In the mid-twentieth century, doctors became concerned with rising rates of skin cancer. Further investigation revealed that the layer of ozone in the atmosphere, which protects Earth from the destructive ultraviolet rays of the sun, was thinning. Stronger ultraviolet radiation was destroying the cells in people's skin, and the result was a deadly form of cancer.

The effect of ozone depletion is strongest in the Southern Hemisphere because the continent of Antarctica is so cold. However, the cause comes from the Northern Hemisphere. There, chemicals called PCBs escape into the atmosphere as a result of the use of refrigerants and spray cans in the populous and wealthy countries. Under a treaty signed in Montreal in 1975, use of these chemicals has declined, and the hole in the ozone has begun to fill in. Furthermore, the Australian government has mounted a campaign to teach people to protect themselves from the harmful rays of the sun: "Slip (on a shirt), slap (on a hat), and slop (on sunscreen)." Nevertheless, the topic of ozone depletion continues to be a concern, not only in Australia but elsewhere in the world as well.

The effects of global warming concern the entire region. Human activities that add carbon dioxide and other gases caused by burning fossil fuels to the atmosphere contribute to global warming. The cutting down of forests, which absorb carbon dioxide, does as well. In Papua New Guinea, tropical forests are being cut for their valuable timber. Scientists have found that because of global warming, glaciers and ice caps around the world are melting. If such human activities continue unchecked, a rise in sea level will result, as this water flows into the oceans. Such a rise in sea level could mean the end of many low-lying islands, as they sink beneath the ocean's rising surface. It could also mean the flooding of coastal land in other areas—and remember that most of Australia's and New Zealand's people live along the coast.

Australians and New Zealanders are environmentally conscious. They understand that their plants and animals are unique in the world, and they have seen the devastating results of introducing new species, like rabbits, in Australia. Both countries have nature preserves and take precautions to prevent new species from entering their countries.

CULTURES

All countries in this region had inhabitants and their many distinctive cultures long before Europeans arrived. These indigenous people had developed adaptations to their environments, for which the European latecomers had little or no respect. Indigenous people died of European diseases, warfare, and general cultural destruction. In some places, Europeans aggravated the conflict among the indigenous groups. In the last 100 years or so, countries in this region have received immigrants from non-European countries. As a result, many of these countries face the continuing challenge of maintaining good relations among different cultural groups.

Comprising about one percent of its population, Australia's Aborigines continue to suffer discrimination and lower standards of living than other groups. How to help them enjoy better education, health, and social services while strengthening their traditional culture remains a goal. In New Zealand, the Maori make up almost 10 percent of the population. Although these indigenous people are more assimilated into mainstream New Zealand culture than are their Australian counterparts, on average their standard of living still lags behind that of the Pakeha, or white New Zealanders. A particular thorny issue is Maori land claims under the Treaty of Waitangi; other people, most of whom are European in origin, today live on that land that the native Maori believe belongs to them.

Even the small islands of the Pacific have cultural conflicts. Some of the island groups included more than one ethnic group before European settlement. Europeans brought in other foreign groups to work on plantations. On Fiji, the indigenous population was a mixture of Melanesian and Polynesian, as the island sits on the boundary between the two regions. Then came

Europeans, and they brought South Asian plantation workers. South Asians, barred from owning land, went into business and today dominate much of the commerce of the country.

ECONOMY

The main exports of all these countries are products of farm, mine, and forest that will be made into finished goods in other countries. Such dependence on far-off markets for these products can be precarious. For example, a major export of Australia and New Zealand is wool. After World War II, synthetic textiles such as polyester and acrylic began to replace wool in manufacturing clothing and blankets. Polyester and acrylic fabrics are washable and therefore are easy to care for. The market for wool declined. Similarly, many of the Pacific islands export coconut and palm oil, which are widely used in baking. Scientists have recently discovered that these oils raise cholesterol levels and therefore are unhealthy. As are result, they are less in demand and the islands lost their market.

Tourism also depends on conditions far from the places to which tourists might come. Long-distance jet airplanes have placed the Pacific islands, as well as Australia and New Zealand, within range of Europe, North America, and Japan. They have also eliminated the need for refueling locations on the Pacific islands, however. Furthermore, tourism can suffer from economic recessions in the tourists' home countries and from fear of travel after attacks by terrorists.

All the countries in Australia and the Pacific must adapt to changes in the demand for their products and services in other parts of the world. Some changes may cause pain initially, such as when factories close. Residents must be flexible and be ready to learn to do different types of work.

POLITICS

Environmental, cultural, and economic issues rapidly become political issues. Groups of people have different interests and see different ways of solving problems—preferably with minimal damage to their own ways of life and prosperity.

Traditionally, Australia has had more ties to the United States than New Zealand has. The country has joined the United States in both the Vietnam War and the invasion of Iraq. During the Vietnam War, soldiers spent their rest and recreation ("R and R") leaves in Australia and were warmly welcomed. From time to time, Australians debate whether to break ties to the British monarch and become a republic, with a president as head of state. The last time this debate came up was in the late 1990s, with the advocates of a republic wanting to make the change before the 2000 Olympic Games in Sydney. However, the idea was defeated, and Australia still recognizes the British Queen as its head of state.

New Zealand is more tied to the British monarchy and to date has not shown any interest in becoming a republic. Like Australia, its flag includes the British Union Jack in the upper left-hand corner. Nevertheless, it tends to be independent in its foreign policy, declining to join the invasion of Iraq and declaring itself a nuclear-free zone.

Relations among different cultural groups in the Pacific islands occasionally boil over into armed rebellion as groups jockey for position. These newly independent countries are still working on the best way to accommodate all points of view democratically. Fiji has seen several governments overthrown by conflicts that involve culture and economic privilege. Samoa also has seen armed conflict, and Australia sent peacekeeping forces there in 2003.

Australia and the Pacific are still as far away from the centers of power in the United States and Europe as you can get on planet Earth. Flying across the Pacific Ocean is long and tedious—it's a big ocean that, at the equator, spans half the globe. However, faster transportation and communications technology have "shrunk" this distance, not in miles or kilometers, but in time required to span the distance. You can now talk to

The Queen of England, in a cloak of kiwi feathers, receives a Maori welcome at the Marae in Christchurch, New Zealand. Continuing its close ties with the British monarchy, New Zealand has not shown any interest in becoming a republic. Nevertheless, it tends to be independent in its foreign policy, declining to join the invasion of Iraq and declaring itself to be a nuclear-free zone.

someone there on the telephone or e-mail them with instantaneous delivery. The 2000 Olympics were broadcast by satellite hookup all over the world. These kinds of links have brought this region more firmly into the world orbit of economic and political life. Its people have recognized the importance of their location for over 200 years, as they relied on trade to make a living. They will continue to feel the effects of "globalization" in the twenty-first century.

About 40,000 years ago	The first people settle Australia from Southeast Asia.
9000 B.C.	Farming begins on New Guinea.
A.D. 700–1000	Polynesians settle New Zealand, the last Pacific island group to be populated.
1520–1521	Ferdinand Magellan sails across the Pacific Ocean to the Philippines, where he is killed; his crew returns to Spain, completing the first round-the-world voyage.
1768–1779	Captain James Cook makes three voyages to Australia, New Zealand, and the Pacific islands.
1788	The First Fleet of convicts and guards arrives in Australia.
1789–1790	Mutiny on the *Bounty* leads to settlement of Pitcairn Island.
About 1802	Whale and seal hunters began settlements in New Zealand.
1840	Treaty of Waitangi grants British rule over New Zealand.
1851	Gold is discovered near Bathurst, New South Wales, leading to Australia's first gold rush.
Late 1800s	Britain and France, joined later by Germany, take most of the Pacific islands as colonies.
1901	Australia becomes a dominion in the British Empire.
1907	New Zealand becomes a dominion in the British Empire.
1914–1918	Australians and New Zealanders fight with British forces in World War I.
1930s	Worldwide depression reduces markets for Australian and New Zealand goods.
1930s	Japan expands its possessions in the Pacific.
1939–1945	Australian and New Zealand forces fight for Britain in World War II; with many important battles, Allied forces retake Japanese-held Pacific islands.
1956	Melbourne, Australia, hosts the Olympics.
1960–1994	Most Pacific islands achieve independence.
1986	New Zealand declares itself a nuclear-free zone.
1988	Australia celebrates the bicentennial of the First Fleet and dedicates its new Parliament building in Canberra.
2000	Sydney, Australia, hosts the Olympics.

Aplin, Graeme. *Australians and Their Environment.* Melbourne, Australia: Oxford University Press, 2002.

Baedeker New Zealand. New York: Macmillan Travel, 1997.

Bonn, David, ed. *Uluru Stories*, 2nd ed. Alice Springs, Australia: Tanami Press, 2001.

Britton, Steve, Richard LeHeron, and Eric Pawson. *Changing Places in New Zealand: A Geography of Restructuring.* Christchurch, New Zealand: New Zealand Geographical Society, 1993.

Bryson, Bill. *In a Sunburned Country.* New York: Broadway Books, 2001.

Burenhult, Goran, gen. ed. *The First Humans: Human Origins and History to 10,000 B.C.* San Francisco: HarperSanFrancisco, 1993.

Burenhult, Goran, gen. ed. *Traditional Peoples Today: Continuity and Change in the Modern World.* San Francisco: HarperSanFrancisco, 1994.

Hanna, Nick. *Exploring New Zealand.* New York: Random House, 2001.

Harrell, Mary Ann. *Surprising Lands Down Under.* Washington, DC: National Geographic Society, 1989.

Head, Leslie. *Second Nature: The History and Implications of Australia as Aboriginal Landscape.* Syracuse, NY: Syracuse University Press, 2000.

Horwitz, Tony. *Blue Latitudes: Boldly Going Where Captain Cook Has Gone Before.* New York: Henry Holt and Company, 2002.

Hughes, Robert. *The Fatal Shore: The Epic of Australia's Founding.* New York: Alfred A. Knopf, 1987.

Johnson, Marael, and Andrew Hampstead. *Australia Handbook.* Emeryville, CA: Avalon Travel Publishing, 2000.

King, Jane. *New Zealand Handbook.* Chico, CA: Moon Publications, 1993.

Knightley, Philip. *Australia: A Biography of a Nation.* London: Jonathan Cape, 2000.

McKenzie, D.W., ed. *Heinemann New Zealand Atlas.* Auckland, New Zealand: Heinemann, 1993.

Menkhorst, Peter. *A Field Guide to the Mammals of Australia.* Oxford: Oxford University Press, 2001.

Morcombe, Michael K. *Australian Marsupials and Other Native Mammals.* Melbourne, Australia: Lansdowne Press, 1972.

Nile, Richard, and Christian Clerk. *Cultural Atlas of Australia, New Zealand and the South Pacific.* New York: Facts on File, 1996.

O'Connor, Kevin, Robert Stimson, and Maurice Daly. *Australia's Changing Economic Geography: A Society Dividing.* Melbourne, Australia: Oxford University Press, 2001.

Rose, Deborah Bird. *Nourishing Terrains: Australian Aboriginal Views of Landscape and Wilderness.* Canberra: Australian Heritage Commission, 1996.

Rutland, Suzanne D. *Edge of the Diaspora: Two Centuries of Jewish Settlement in Australia.* New York: Holmes & Meier, 1997.

Searle, E.J. *City of Volcanoes: A Geology of Auckland,* new ed., rev. by R. D. Mayhill. Auckland, New Zealand: Longman Paul, 1981.

Sinclaire, Keith. *A History of New Zealand,* 4th rev. ed. Auckland, New Zealand: Penguin Books, 1991.

Stanley, David. *Moon Handbooks: Fiji,* 6th ed. Emeryville, CA: Avalon Travel Publishing, 2001.

Sturman, Andrew, and Nigel Tapper. *The Weather and Climate of Australia and New Zealand.* Melbourne, Australia: Oxford University Press, 1996.

Sturman, Andrew, and Rachel Spronken-Smith, eds. *The Physical Environment: A New Zealand Perspective.* Melbourne, Australia: Oxford University Press, 2001.

ADDITIONAL SOURCES:

Field work in Australia, New Zealand, and Fiji, summer 2003; newspapers, magazines, pamphlets, papers delivered at the New Zealand Geographical Society meetings, Auckland, July 2003.

BOOKS

Bartlett, Anne. *The Aboriginal Peoples of Australia.* Minneapolis: Lerner, 2002.

Birkett, Bill, ed. *Classic Treks: The 30 Most Spectacular Hikes in the World.* Boston: Little, Brown, 2000.

Burenhult, Goran, ed. *The First Humans: Human Origins and History to 10,000 B.C.* San Francisco: HarperSanFrancisco, 1993.

Burenhult, Goran, ed. *Traditional Peoples Today: Continuity and Change in the Modern World.* San Francisco: HarperSanFrancisco, 1994.

Burt, Jocelyn. *Australia's Outback: Journeys and Discoveries.* Boston: Houghton Mifflin, 1992.

Coleman, Neville. *Australia's Great Barrier Reef.* Secaucus, NJ: Chartwell Books, 1990.

Collins, Alan. *Jacob's Ladder.* New York: Lodestar, 1989.

Crew, Gary. *No Such Country.* New York: Simon and Schuster Books for Young Readers, 1993.

Disher, Garry. *The Divine Wind: A Love Story.* New York: A.A. Levine, 2002.

Fisher, Ronald M. *Wild Shores of Australia.* Washington, DC: National Geographic Society, 1996.

Gascoigne, Toss, ed. *Dream Time: New Stories by Sixteen Award-winning Authors.* Boston: Houghton Mifflin, 1991.

Gillespie, Carol Ann. *New Zealand (Modern World Nations).* Philadelphia: Chelsea House Publishers, 2002.

Harrell, Mary Ann. *Surprising Lands Down Under.* Washington, DC: National Geographic Society, 1989.

Hausman, Gerald and Loretta. *Escape from Botany Bay: The True Story of Mary Bryant.* New York: Orchard Books, 2003.

Horizon Magazine. *Captain Cook and the South Pacific.* New York: American Heritage Publishing Company, 1963.

Jackson, Donald Dale. *Kangaroos and Other Creatures from Down Under.* New York: Time-Life Films, 1977.

Jonsen, Helen. *Kangaroo's Comments and Wallaby's Words: The Aussie Word Book.* New York: Hippocrene Books, 1988.

Jordan-Bychkov, Terry. *Australia (Modern World Nations).* Philadelphia: Chelsea House Publishers, 2004.

Matthews, Graeme. *The Edge of the Land: The Coastline of New Zealand.* Christchurch, New Zealand, and London: Whitcoulis, 1983.

McGregor, Craig. *The Great Barrier Reef.* Amsterdam: Time-Life Books, 1974.

Meisel, Jacqueline Drobis. *Australia: The Land Down Under.* New York: Benchmark, 1998.

Meltzer, Milton. *Captain James Cook.* New York: Benchmark Books/Marshall Cavendish, 2002.

Menkhorst, Peter. *A Field Guide to the Mammals of Australia.* Melbourne, Australia: Oxford University Press, 2001.

Morcombe, Michael K. *Australia Marsupials and Other Native Animals.* Melbourne, Australia: Lansdowne Press, 1972.

Moriarty, Jaclyn. *Feeling Sorry for Celia.* New York: St. Martin's Press, 2001.

Morris, Rod. *South Sea Islands: A Natural History.* Toronto: Firefly Books, 2003.

Pilkington, Doris. *Rabbit-proof Fence.* New York: Hyperion, 2002.

Pople, Maureen. *A Nugget of Gold.* New York: H. Holt, 1988.

Vandenbled, John. *Nature of Australia: A Portrait of the Island Continent.* New York: Facts on File, 1988.

WEBSITES

About Australia
www.about-australia.com

Australian Aboriginals
www.crystalinks.com/aboriginals.html

Australian Government: Geoscience Australia
www.ga.gov.au/

Guide to Australia
www.csu.edu.au/Australia

Official Site of the Maori
www.maori.org.nz

INDEX

INDEX

PICTURE CREDITS

page:

2: © Elizabeth J. Leppman
3: © Mapping Specialists, Ltd.
11: New Millennium Images
12: New Millennium Images
16: © Mapping Specialists, Ltd.
21: © Geoff Moon; Frank Lane Picture Agency/CORBIS
26: New Millennium Images
31: New Millennium Images
43: © Mapping Specialists, Ltd.
47: © Elizabeth J. Leppman
51: © Elizabeth J. Leppman
58: © Paul A. Saunders/CORBIS
63: Associated Press, AP
69: Associated Press, AP/Rob Griffith
74: KRT/New Millennium Images
76: © Mapping Specialists, Ltd.
79: © Kevin Fleming/CORBIS
84: KRT/New Millennium Images
92: © Elizabeth J. Leppman
94: New Millennium Images
101: The Sun/News International Photos/New Millennium Images
Cover: New Millennium Images

ELIZABETH J. LEPPMAN has taught geography at St. Cloud State University in Minnesota. She has also taught in Pennsylvania, Georgia, and Ohio, and she has taught English in China. She has lived and traveled in many countries, including Australia, New Zealand, and Fiji and conducts research and writes about culture, especially food, religion, and politics. Elizabeth has served as editor of the *Journal of Geography*, a publication about teaching geography, and is the author of *Teaching Map and Globe Skills: A Handbook* (Rand McNally, 1982) and *Changing Rice Bowl: Economic Development and Diet in China* (Hong Kong University Press, 2005), and co-author of *Pennsylvania Dutch Country: A Pictorial History* (Pennsylvania Publishers, 1986) and *Student Atlas of World Politics*, 6th edition (Dushkin/McGraw-Hill, 2004).

CHARLES F. ("FRITZ") GRITZNER is Distinguished Professor of Geography at South Dakota University in Brookings. He is now in his fifth decade of college teaching and research. During his career, he has taught more than 60 different courses, spanning the fields of physical, cultural, and regional geography. In addition to his teaching, he enjoys writing, working with teachers, and sharing his love for geography with students. As consulting editor for the MODERN WORLD NATIONS series, he has a wonderful opportunity to combine each of these "hobbies." Fritz has served as both President and Executive Director of the National Council for Geographic Education and has received the Council's highest honor, the George J. Miller Award for Distinguished Service. In March 2004, he won the Distinguished Teaching award from the American Association of Geographers at their annual meeting held in Philadelphia.